Engaging the Immediate

Engaging the Immediate

Applying Kierkegaard's Theory
of Indirect Communication
to the Practice of Psychotherapy

Katherine M. Ramsland

Lewisburg
Bucknell University Press
London and Toronto: Associated University Presses

Associated University Presses
440 Forsgate Drive
Cranbury, NJ 06512

Associated University Presses
25 Sicilian Avenue
London WC1A 2QH, England

Associated University Presses
P.O. Box 488, Port Credit
Mississauga, Ontario
Canada L5G 4M2

The paper used in this publication meets the requirements of the American National Standard for Permanence of Paper for Printed Library Materials Z39.48-1984.

Library of Congress Cataloging-in-Publication Data
Ramsland, Katherine M., 1953–
  Engaging the immediate.

  Bibliography: p.
  Includes index.
  1. Psychotherapy. 2. Psychotherapy patients
—Language. I. Kierkegaard, Soren, 1813–1855.
II. Title. [DNLM: 1. Communication. 2. Psycho-
therapy—methods.   WM 420 R183e]
RC489.P73R36   1989   616.89'14'01   87-46432
ISBN 0-8387-5152-0 (alk. paper)

Printed in the United States of America

FOR DEWEY

Contents

Preface   9

1 Introduction   13
2 Objectivity in Theory and Therapy   24
3 Human Possibility and Metaphor   56
4 Kierkegaard's Indirect Communication   75
5 Applications to Therapy   92
6 Conclusion   114

References   125
Index   131

Preface

Although essentially philosophical, this work is intended primarily for clinical psychologists who recognize the limitations of objectivity and who seek a rationale with which to move beyond a predominantly objective approach to their clients. I have attempted to provide a philosophical context for those who already use some or all of the techniques suggested, as well as to motivate those who do not use such techniques to ponder the possibilities for the clinical situation.

The purpose of this book is to explore the various ways in which the objective content of human experience is separated from theories; to show how such approaches can be detrimental in the practice of counseling; and to examine the approach of the philosopher Søren Kierkegaard, which focuses on the ongoing experiencing of individuals, both that of a person who may be the target of theoretical analysis (e.g., a client in therapy) and that of the theorist (e.g., the therapist). Objective theories that focus on the content of human experience to the neglect and sometimes even to the exclusion of the individual's lived engagement in the world dominate clinical practice. Since I cannot deal with all of the available theories, I present a survey of several prominent theories that represent the typical modes of objectivity by which clinicians are often influenced.

Because of the elusive nature of subjectivity, objectivity has become a prejudice and a dogma in many clinical circles. While I do not intend to stigmatize any one method of therapy, I do want to depict basic attitudes that make clinicians of any persuasion vulnerable to objectivist tendencies. Those theories that take objectivity to an extreme will inevitably be hardest hit by the criticisms. However, the discussion is intended not as a polemic but as an attempt to reveal how clinical perspectives restricted by objectivist prejudices can impede effective therapy insofar as they encourage a neglect of—even a failure to see—clinical phenomena that are not included as human phenomena by the biases in question.

For the purposes of this work, the clinical situation, briefly described, will be viewed as consisting of at least one therapist, at least one client, and the topics and modes of communication between them. Other forms of therapy may vary from this basic model, but the discussion is applicable to any therapeutic form in which there are at least two participants. It is assumed that the client has come (or been brought) with a psychological need, and that the therapist views his or her task as that of applying his or her knowledge or skill to detect and to meet or correct that need. While I do not attempt an exhaustive analysis of the clinical situation, I do intend to pinpoint a key weakness in the predominant approaches in clinical psychology. I also intend to offer a means of rectifying that weakness.

I wish to thank Bruce Wilshire, George Atwood, Dorothea Frede, and Brian McLaughlin at Rutgers University for their assistance in reading this work. My special thanks to Bruce Wilshire, who guided me past my own mental boundaries into new areas of thought.

The study incorporates excerpts from Søren Kierkegaard, *Concluding Unscientific Postscript*, trans. David F. Swenson and Walter Lowrie. Copyright 1941 © 1969 by Princeton University Press. Excerpts reprinted with permission of Princeton University Press.

Engaging the Immediate

1
Introduction

Macbeth. Canst thou not minister to a mind diseased,
   Pluck from the memory a rooted sorrow,
   Raze out the written troubles of the brain,
   And with some sweet oblivious antedote,
   Cleanse the stuff'd bosom of that perilous stuff
   Which weighs upon the heart?
Doctor. Therein the patient
   Must minister to himself.

—Shakespeare, *Macbeth*

In a prison camp during one Easter week, Feodor Dostoevsky withdrew in disgust from his fellow prisoners. Many of the men were drunk, singing lewd songs and gambling. Miserable, having witnessed the brutal beating of an unpopular inmate, Dostoevsky ran from the Russian barracks "like a madman." He began to walk around the yard to calm his indignation and rancor. He happened to encounter another prisoner out walking, a Polish man. "He looked at me gloomily, his eyes flashed and his lips began trembling: '*Je hais ces brigands* [I hate these bandits]!' he muttered through clenched teeth in a half strangled voice, and passed by" (Dostoevsky [1876], 1979, 206).

Stricken by the other man's words and attitude, Dostoevsky returned immediately to his barracks. It was as if the Pole had read his mind, had spewed out his own vile thoughts. He saw himself mirrored in the other man; he saw how he had separated himself from his fellow Russians. It gave him a terrible jolt. His heart beat fast, and the seething words rang in his ears. It was a momentous event in his life, as he later recorded in his diary. The incident provoked childhood memories of a loving, protective gesture from a serf on his father's estate. His abrupt return to the barracks—to the place he had most wanted to avoid—was a gesture of solidarity with his countrymen, a result of swift, forceful insight. "I remember, when I got off the plank bed and gazed around, that I suddenly felt I could look at these unfortunates with quite different eyes, and suddenly, as if by a miracle, all hatred and rancor had vanished from my heart" (Dostoevsky [1876] 1979, 210).

Dostoevsky underwent a basic conversion experience in his beliefs and attitudes about the Russian peasant (Frank 1983). What he had seen in the other grumbling prisoner had provoked a startling discovery of himself, which might otherwise have lain dormant under layers of self-blindness and frustrated moral superiority. In essence, watching his own attitude enacted through the actions of another person showed him an aspect of himself that he detested. Having seen it, he acted to change it.

It does not require such intense inward circumspection as Dostoevsky's for such self-discoveries to occur. The possibilities abound for each of us. A young teacher was told by one of her colleagues that she possessed a nervous laugh. Upon hearing what she took to be a negative description of her buoyant personality, she simply denied it, wrote it off as a superficial interpretation. However, one evening when talking with her sister she heard the echo of her own laugh in her sister's giggle. And her sister had a distinctly nervous laugh! What the teacher had failed to perceive when it was verbally described, she was able to recognize when another person's mannerisms were like hers.

While such insights about ourselves may be available to all of us in a wide variety of contexts, we still may not see past them to ourselves. It sometimes takes a discerning and skillful "outside" person to get the ball rolling.

Philip Barker (1985) tells of twelve-year-old Anne, ordinarily a good student, who had lost motivation for her class work. Her grandmother, with whom she had a close, affectionate relationship, was informed of the situation by Anne's disappointed parents.

Anne visited her grandmother and mentioned how much she detested her social studies course. She could find nothing of interest in it. Anne's grandmother, in the habit of telling the girl interesting stories, sat down and engaged her in a tale about a boy her age named Charles.

This boy lived near the ocean with his parents. They got along very well, except for one problem: Charles's parents took daily walks along the beach and insisted that he join them. He had grown bored with these walks and only agreed to them begrudgingly.

One day, as he was walking along, pouting, he noticed the seashells at his feet. They fascinated him. He collected several and took them home with him.

The next day Charles went to the school library and found a book on shellfish. He took it home and compared the shells he had with the pictures in the book. . . .

Charles. . . became pleased when his parents asked him to go for walks along the shore, as this gave him opportunities to find more shells . . . his walks along the seashore were no longer boring. (Barker 1985, 4–5).

The story Anne's grandmother told her was intended to parallel Anne's situation, to communicate with her without resorting to the lecturing, pleading, or direct confrontations that had proven fruitless for Anne's parents. Gradually, over a few months, Anne began to make better progress in school. Whether or not it was the message in the story that had made a positive difference in Anne's attitude, the potential was present to do so. At a symbolic level, Anne was encouraged to look for something she might learn even in a situation she did not enjoy.

Like Dostoevsky, like the young teacher, like Anne, we are all prone to possible blindness to facets of our behavior or personality. Some of us dislike characteristics in others that are similar to our own (though we might deny that they are, indeed, like our own). A boisterous person is antagonized by another such person. Pompous or dogmatic people tend to react negatively to others like them. The over-confident tennis player might be surprised to hear an observation about his clumsiness. We can fail to grasp the immediacy of our lived involvement in the world when we are so engulfed in it that we fail to focus on it, or when we are put off by it, perhaps embarrassed to acknowledge it as our own.

The therapist sees this phenomenon of benign self-deception on a daily basis. How it is handled, however, varies from therapist to therapist. It is possible, through well-meaning but ineffectective treatment, to push clients further into their debilitating myopia. What the therapist may need for effective intervention is a fuller grasp of the functions of communication in the specific context of obscured or truncated experiencing. Simply to articulate the problem for the client in straightfoward language—the most immediately accessible approach—may short-circuit the therapy. A more effective procedure—sometimes even for those clients for whom direct articulation works well enough—would call on the various methods of indirect communication.

Indirect communication typically involves metaphor, which has the potential to convey multiple meanings. Embedded sometimes in stories, sometimes in objects, sometimes simply in the behavior or expressions of another person, enough similarity is evident in the metaphor to allow clients to note parallels to their own experiencing. Typically, this form of recognition is intuitive and visceral rather than cognitive, a possibility granted in virtue of the structure of consciousness.

Each moment of consciousness is at least as much marginal as it is focused. That is, awareness feathers out to fuzzy boundaries so that only some things stand out in a thematic way while other things provide a nonintrusive, subconsciously noted background. For example, two women conducted an interview in a room in which the air conditioning unit was noisy but not so obtrusive that they were aware of it. One woman became increasingly irritated as she strained to hear the other, but she attributed her irritation to something in the other woman's manner. The noise of the air conditioner remained in the background; it fed into her perceptions, but not in a manner that drew her explicit attention.

In Gestalt terminology, figure stands out only in contrast to this background: we need a wall against which to see a chair. We can locate the building in which our dentist is waiting although we may not be able even to name the surrounding buildings that make its location significant to us. That is, much of our perception is peripheral. We take in the perceptible milieu, it contributes to our store of learnings, but we are not explicitly aware of everything that we perceive in day-to-day encounters.

The fluid nature of consciousness is derived from the continuity at the fuzzy borders, the moment-by-moment flow of peripheral perceptions that feeds into our awareness but does not draw our explicit attention. This characteristic of consciousness allows a sense of ourselves that, like perception, feathers out and becomes vague; it may even be eclipsed altogether by aspects of our character or behavior that more forcefully elicit our conscious attention. It is possible, as shown in the examples above, to be engaged in an activity in a particular manner without being fully aware of it at all! Just as I might realize I have blue eyes only when I look into a mirror or hear the fact from another person, I can be blind to some feature of my personality in which I am so closely involved that I fail to see it. When the limitations of self-awareness become a stumbling block to adjustment or to growth, I need a device that will allow a fuller perception of myself, like the prisoner for Dostoevsky, or the sister for the young teacher.

Consciousness carries no clear sense of itself into its typical activities. While engaged in a given activity, we might miss much of *how* we are engaged because the "how" is hidden in the flow of the *process* of being engaged. We could attempt to step back to reflect on consciousness itself and try to delineate actively the boundaries of consciousness—to bring it more fully into a reflective focus and thus expand our explicit awareness—but while involved in this procedure we cannot avoid the loss of the background flow that makes *this* activity possible. There will always be some unreflected reflecting, and thus some part of experiencing will elude explicit awareness. The important question is whether something crucial to self-understanding is lost. The preceding cases suggest it seems altogether likely.

A great deal of clinical data suggests that conscious reflection on human experience misses something. Even the most articulate, reflective clients can perceive themselves in such a way that positive changes are blocked rather than facilitated; they may know how and why they are hindered but still be unable to act on that knowledge. Even if cognitive reflection were able to provide accurate data about our experiencing—to give us clear, succinct, descriptive sentences about ourselves—such accuracy does not give us the visceral quality of our lived engagements. To say that I am angry does little to convey the full-bodied quality of my emotional state. This qualitative difference between *how* we are experienc*ing* and *what* we can say that we have experienc*ed* points to the probability that conscious reflection is a mediating activity at best that, in all likelihood, alters if not misses altogether the brute qualities of our lived encounters in the world.

This fact has important implications for therapy. If clients can be ignorant of, or unable to act on, aspects of their behavior that foul them up, then they need an awareness that will give them back to themselves, viscerally. Their *lived* sense of their experiencing, not just their insight, needs to be expanded: "Insight—the logical understanding of a situation—is of little value in itself. Understanding *why* you are behaving or feeling a particular way does not usually help you to behave or feel differently" (Barker 1985, 21). This is especially true for persons who have actually disowned something of their experience in such a way that *only* "coming up on them from behind" through something other than direct linguistic articulation will be of any use.

Milton Erickson, a psychiatrist noted for hypnotic therapy and "teaching tales," offered a good example of a therapeutic intervention that circumvented linguistic diagnosis and instruction in his story about two psychotic clients who both claimed to be Jesus Christ. It would be difficult, from the position of a limited mortal, to inform Jesus Christ that he was not who he said he was. He, after all, is God. Noting this, Erickson put the two "Christs" on a bench together and instructed each of them to explain to the other who the real Jesus Christ was. After a month, one of them said, "I'm saying the same things as that crazy fool is saying. He's crazy and I'm saying what he says. That must mean I'm crazy, too; and I don't want to be crazy" (Rosen 1982, 201). The patient became aware of the other "impersonator" and noted something about himself that he might not have gained had Erickson simply said, "It's crazy to think you're Jesus Christ." This realization was this patient's first step toward eventually gaining freedom from his psychotic identifications.

Metaphorical devices have been used in a variety of contexts, from teaching to counseling. They have the advantage of suggesting without directly confronting, of mirroring without provoking defensive guards. "Therapeutic metaphors offer new choices, especially new ways of looking at things, and can tap a variety of experiences, beliefs and ideas that have been dormant in the listener's mind" (Barker 1985, 13). Metaphors are ambiguous in their symbolism and are thus flexible in what they can mean to the recipient. They can enhance a therapeutic relationship by provoking interest and increasing rapport.

The general understanding of metaphorical communication is that it has the power to communicate with the unconscious or preconscious mind, i.e., to speak the same imagistic, symbolic language as that which occupies the ambiguous margins of our consciousness, where many of our resources and learnings are stored (Erickson 1980). If a dream can, through symbol, reveal something of that enigmatic part of our minds, it is reasonable to suppose that we, also through some sort of mimetic symbol, can communicate back. And since the symbol is ostensibly "about something else," as the grandmother's story was "about Charles," the intended message is not as readily blocked by defensive postures as an explicit reference to our "shortcomings" might be. People often can see, through indirect symbolic communication, what they may not acknowledge when told the same thing directly. For example, direct verbal reprimands and entreaties from Anne's parents had had no obvious effect on her. She had instead resisted them with further involvement in the undesirable behavior.

With techniques of therapy that utilize experiential mirrors, e.g., metaphorical stories, the client's manner of participating in his or her world often can be made evident to the individual more quickly and effectively. One of the goals of therapy should be to help clients reengage themselves with themselves—to grasp something of *how* they are involved, not just *what* those involvements are. "Psychotherapy is essentially a process of providing people with more choice in the matter of how they behave or respond emotionally in various situations . . . of helping people to see things differently and to feel differently about them" (Basker 1985, 17). The difference in therapy between simply *telling* a client what is wrong or what to do or who he or she is, and using a device that will *show* them is the difference between seeing pictures of various stages of a river and watching it in action. Words as reference or as names tend to categorize and fragment the flow of experiencing into discretely divided experiences. They chop into it like a cookie cutter, isolating out that which can be explicitly referred to and leaving behind the excess dough. However, when words are used simply as building blocks for symbolic devices, as in a parable, language is employed for developing living imagery and meaning—*indirect* communication. It can spark the immediacy of experiencing and have greater potential to help clients reengage with their lived sense of their situation—put them at the river's edge.

> There are thus two languages involved. The one, in which, for instance this sentence itself is expressed, is objective, definitional, cerebral, logical, analytic; it is the language of reason, of science, explanation and interpretation, and therefore the language of most psychotherapy. The other . . . is much more difficult to define—precisely because it is not the language of definition. We might call it the language of imagery, or metaphor . . . perhaps of symbols, but certainly of synthesis and totality, and not of analytical dissection. (Watzlawick 1978, 14–15)

For example, in the situation described earlier, the young teacher was told she had a nervous laugh. The label not only put her off but gave her only a cognitive grasp of the named characteristic. She acknowledged the meaning but failed to perceive its application to her own experience. However, when the nervous laugh was *mirrored* to her, it touched her experientially. She heard the laugh as an echo of her own. The communication bypassed a strictly cognitive apprehension because of the full-bodied, experiential *feel* of the nervous characteristic in her sister's laughing. Hearing it in another did more to communicate to her the wholeness of her behavior than having it named to her.

Direct, objective, linguistic communication gives the illusion that there is an Archimedian point from which human beings can step out of their experiencing and grasp it in complete objectivity—by naming it. However, this is like believing one can hold a river by sticking one's hands in it. There will always be, as Kierkegaard ([1846] 1968) says, some part of the experiential process—the "how" or subjective mode of our experiencing—that cannot be caught up entirely in the "what," or verbally expressible content.

It is to the advantage of practicing clinicians to achieve and maintain the most productive exchange possible between themselves and their clients. There is no question that direct communication provides some sense of order and control in the therapeutic situation—when we can name things, we can categorize, generalize, make ourselves understood through language—but naming also tends to divide continuous experiencing into discrete units and thus to short-change the clinical situation. It is the client's interested concern in his or her own experiencing that should be a focal point for the therapist, not how well the symptoms can be articulated, categorized, and analyzed. Explicit verbal expression can fail, on some level, to really communicate to the clients what they might need to realize about themselves. When clients are blocked from recognizing part of their own experiencing *as their own*, the therapist is instrumental in this communication. The therapist, then, must be open to whatever will work best to bring the client into self-awareness.

Although many clinical books about this sort of creative communication are available, few touch on the nature of subjectivity with any theoretical rigor. It is the purpose of this book to fill in these gaps. Rather than discuss how to develop metaphors or list inspiring examples of how such treatment has been effective, the following chapters approach indirect communication through the philosophical analysis of the human condition detailed by Søren Kierkegaard.

Kierkegaard describes the way in which a person can serve as a needed mirror to another (e.g., a therapist to a client) by drawing the recipients, without the mediation of direct communication, into their own personal and concretely individual involvement with their thoughts and experiences. Kierkegaard introduces this possibility by first analyzing the problems inherent in overly abstract approaches to the human condition to which contemporary personality theories are prone. He objects to the empty, ordered logic of such positions, pointing out how an extreme objectivistic attitude (one so concerned with order and system that it disallows the possibility that any facet of human experiencing can elude being pinned down by propositions) results in an impoverished account of—and related-ness to—human existence.

His objections are applicable to clinical approaches that suffer from the same biases toward logical systems and reductionistic order at the cost of elusive human experience. In therapy, this "absent-mindedness"—a failure to recognize the inherent subjectivity of any human viewpoint—is a form of self-deception on the part of the therapist: a self that can forget itself can hardly offer assistance to a self that is blinded to itself. Therapy is the interfacing of two subjectivities. Each is aware of the other from various levels, yet neither is aware of the totality of their immediate experiencing. Neurotic self-detachment or self-cowardice is only aggravated by a distancing, fragmenting approach. Chapter 2 details the problems with an overreliance on objectivity in therapeutic contexts by analyzing the features of human consciousness that promote objective approaches.

Kierkegaard's concern is for the primacy of existing before knowing (Evans 1977). He draws our attention to the fact that although objectivity has its place in the apprehension of human existence, the peripheral areas of our involvement in the world can be entirely eclipsed by that which draws explicitly verbalized conscious focus. In a therapeutic context, clients can be so engrossed in their symptoms that they fail to perceive the background from which the symptom emerges. *They are not experiencing their own experiences fully.* If a therapist approaches clients with theories and devices that further obscure or truncate the clients' experiential world, and those clients already possess only a partial sense of themselves, therapy magnifies rather than relieves or resolves the problem. Clients must somehow be made aware of the fuller subjective background of their experiencing—to see their condition as one human possibility among others and not as a necessary reality. If objective modes of abstraction and generalization fail to do the trick, the therapist must rely on something else.

Kierkegaard goes on to present a means by which we can tap into the subjective qualities of our experiencing. He describes a technique that he calls double reflection, which is a manner of reflecting on our inner lives in a way that bypasses the structured mediation of literal articulation. According to Kierkegaard, a person reflects both outwardly and inwardly. Outward reflection is akin to the objective type of thinking that turns experiencing into products, that translates human enterprise into words. The inward reflection links the words to the existence from which they were drawn: individuals realize, in a visceral way, the manner in which they are involved in their "thinking about." It is an immediate awareness that discloses the experiencing intuitively as it eludes the objectively reflective grasp. There is no linguistic expression for the second reflection because it is in the form of continuous process. The second reflection accesses that part of our experiencing that is forced into the shadows of the first reflection—the background for articulate awareness. It is the medium for metaphor, and thus sets up the second device that

Kierkegaard proposes for active self-awareness: indirect communication. Kierkegaard advocates disclosing as much as possible the "how" of our experiencing by symbolically dilating the "what." We should grasp how thought-products are related to the particular here-and-now of the thinking individual. We can then see how theories and beliefs reveal, to some degree, a person's own manner of engagement in the world. And since words as reference that point to *an experience* cannot contain the whole of the fluid experienc*ing*, Kierkegaard develops a technique of indirect communication to touch into the elusive, subjectively formed, visceral fluidity of experiencing. He offers a way to engage in an active self-penetration that alerts us to the fact that there is something within our own experiencing to perceive, without telling us exactly *what*. This approach brings us close to our phenomenal center, where we experience the freedom to master something, to avoid it, or to decide even to care about it. Kierkegaard requires that we remain in contact with this center as a vital anchoring of our existence.

For therapists, this indirect communication can take many forms, from role-playing to construction of allegories. The point is to direct the clients' attention back to their own involvement in their experiencing, to construct a possible world that will mimic that of the client, in hopes that clients who can view themselves in another world can see the likeness to their own in such a way that they will be referred, viscerally, back to their own. And it is crucial at such times, given that there is no literal translation of the "inward reflection," that these contexts be nonpropositional.

Metaphor is the medium of interpretation. Clients are not told what to make of it. They either see or don't see the application, and if they do see it, chances are they will be jolted back to themselves, as Dostoevsky was, compelled to attach personal meaning to the image presented. The therapist cannot be certain how the metaphor will be taken by the client, but even if it is understood only superficially, or even rejected, less is lost than if solutions had been more straightforwardly presented. It is important that clients discover the truth about themselves *for* themselves and *within* themselves. "Therein must the patient cure himself." Although the common structuring of human experience allows the therapist to perceive that about which clients may be blind or impotent, the actual concrete contents of experiencing are individual and must be allowed the lattitude that individuality demands. A metaphor increases therapeutic flexibility in this regard.

The purpose of the indirect, metaphorical approach is to provoke clients into freeing themselves from the self-obscuration that imprisons them in their particular debilitating symptoms. It can also be employed in situations in which clients are in doubt about solutions, bored, or overintellectualizing (Barker 1985). To experience one's own experience as only possibility rather than as necessity is accomplished through the second reflection (in Kierkegaard's terminology), wherein a client's own relation to the symbol or image is self-established. Viewed as possibility, clients can be attentive to alternatives. The "possible world," such as the world of seashells and new explorations for Anne, puts enough distance between the clients and the immediacy of their situation for them to experience fully their own behavior, attitudes, and mannerisms, as well as to apprehend the solutions proposed in the analogical situations presented by the therapist. As Kierkegaard points out, "When I understand another person, his reality is for me a possibility, and in its aspect of possibility, this conceived reality is related to me as the thought of something I have not done is related to the doing of it" ([1846] 1968, 285). If clients can be made to perceive their own actual situations as possibility, and to perceive how the possible solutions offered may be incorporated into their own realities, then therapy can provoke the first steps toward recovery.

The point, then, is that if the self-blindness endemic in the objectively dominated psychological theories can be corrected with the inclusion of subjectively tolerant indirect communication, it is likely that the self-blindness in clients can be more readily accessed, revealed, and purged.

2
Objectivity in Theory and Therapy

The Objective Bias: Its Development

Therapeutic procedures are usually dictated by theory, and theory by the values of the therapist. Professional values are often dictated by the professional community. Currently the bias toward natural science pressures therapists to formulate concepts and methods by which human subjects can be approached under a predominantly objective orientation. As a result of this pressure, systematic formats, universally applicable methods, and generalizable results characterize theories that organize and guide clinical procedure. This chapter details the central features of this orientation and explores some of the ways in which it can be detrimental to the therapeutic situation.

The concept 'objectivity' has been used with shifting senses. In general, an objective approach involves formulating phenomenal realities into objects for indifferent scrutiny that can be explicitly labeled; the results of an objective analysis are then accessible for generalization and categorization so that they can be fit neatly into a comprehensive explanatory system. For some, objectivity entails grasping a given phenomenon in such a way that it is present to the observer as it would be to any point of view: "Objectivity is anonymous. It is an arbitrary fixation of phenomena that sums up the phenomenal world in concepts" (Shmueli 1971, 108). The personal consciousness of the observer disappears into an objective opaqueness.

For others, objectivity can be drawn subtly into a comprehensive objectivism, which is understood as a means of achieving knowledge about reality by allowing all elements of reality to have an observer-independent status. Reality is purportedly seen from a perspectiveless "god's-eye-view" as purified knowledge. Reality can be known in itself and the objective knower can take a disinterested stance, "from nowhere in particular and from no life form in particular" (Nagel 1979, 208). That is, reality-as-object must be perceived free

of distortions that are inherent in personal perspectives. Richard
Bernstein (1983) offers a good overall definition of objectivism:

> [Objectivism is] the basic conviction that there is or must be some
> permanent, ahistorical matrix or framework to which we can ultimately
> appeal in determining the nature of rationality, knowledge, truth, reality,
> goodness or rightness. An objectivist claims that there is (or must be)
> such a matrix and that the primary task of the philosopher is to discover
> what it is and to support his or her claims to have discovered such a
> matrix with the strongest possible reasons. Objectivism is closely related
> to foundationalism and the search for the Archimedean point. (8)

Objectivity is thus regarded as a property of objects (Deutscher
1983). The experiential point of view of the human subject is shunned
as if it comprises illusion rather than the substance of reality. The
"what"—or content of experience—overshadows the "how"—or
mode of experiencing—to such an extent that the "how" is eventually eclipsed. Deutscher views this approach as essentially an
escape from objectivity in its true form, as a subjective projection of
control, shifting the responsibility for objectivity from ourselves
onto things.

A basic metaphysical distinction is made between "object" and
"subject." The "object" supposedly elicits an unemotional, non-
idiosyncratic, neutral, and valueless perspective that has the power
to separate reality from appearance. The "subject" is limited in
point of view, self-interested, prone to the obscuration of emotion,
and caught up by appearances (Deutscher 1983). Clear standards of
knowledge—the "in-itself" core of reality—are assumed to be
achievable only on the side of the "object." This distinction is the
foundation of the natural sciences; the "subject" is of no concern in
the pursuit of knowledge:

> It is common in discussions of science to regard scientists as a kind of
> Absolute Knower—a completely depersonalized being who makes
> observations, performs experiments, describes facts, invents theories,
> and creates symbolic schemes, and then promptly recedes into the back-
> ground. (Cornelius 1965, 14)

Science seeks laws for associating and predicting facts and reduces
the connections discovered to the smallest number of elements. Precise objective methods are essential in reducing the risk of falling
prey to illusions. Knowledge is restricted to the objective, and this
restriction is supported with the progressive attainment of such
knowledge. Einstein (1950) notes this frame of mind: "the more a

man is imbued with the ordered regularity of all events, the firmer becomes his conviction that there is no room left by the side of this ordered regularity for causes of a different nature" (32). Objectivity is assumed to be sufficiently effective in the pursuit of knowledge, and when it apparently proves to be, the approach to knowledge is gradually restricted to an objective one. *This is objectivism.*

Philosophy, too, has its proponents of objectivism. The move toward abstraction that is separated from persons is outlined by Frege (1970). He proposes that meaning must be graspable by many minds, excluding the experiencing of any particular individual from functioning in the pursuit of meaning. The sense of a thought, he claims, must be distinguishable from psychological factors that might be involved in generating the thought:

> The reference and the sense of a sign are to be distinguished from the associated idea. If the reference of a sign is an object perceivable by the senses, my idea of it is an internal image, arising from memories of sense impressions which I have had, and acts, both internal and external, which I have performed. Such an idea is often saturated with feeling; the clarity of its seperate parts varies and oscillates. . . . The idea is subjective. . . . This constitutes an essential distinction between the idea and the sign's sense, which may be the common property of many and therefore is not a part or a mode of the individual mind. (59)

Frege proposes a "cognitive core" that is distinct from the modes of the individual mind and as such can provide the basis for objective (subject-free) conceptualization.

Many contemporary philosophers have been greatly impressed with Frege's division of thinker and thought and have promoted this approach as the only one worthy of study. British philosopher Michael Dummet (1978) makes such a claim:

> Only with Frege was the proper object of philosophy finally established: namely, first, that the goal of philosophy is the analysis of the structure of *thought*; secondly, that the study of *thought* is to be sharply distinguished from the study of the psychological process of *thinking*; and finally, that the only proper method for analyzing thought consists in the analysis of *language*. (458)

That which is considered appropriate for serious study is restricted to the content of thought as brought forth in language. The objective, then, is that which is accessible to direct linguistic expression.

The achievements in natural science and the developments in philosophy have greatly influenced the field of psychology to move toward objectivity in its practice and even toward objectiv*ism* in its basic orientation. The progress of knowledge is advanced by contributions from all areas of research, and, since knowledge is dominated by objective biases, the contributions are generally expected by the professional community to be objectively gained. Psychology, as the science of humankind, is expected to supply and then rely on objective data for the unification of knowledge gained by other disciplines: a psychologist must formulate general laws and principles of the human condition in order systematically to construct and apply general theories. Clinicians in the field are pressured to feed this approach, to support it with objective evidence.

Yet one of the goals of therapy is to gain as much comprehension of the human situation as possible. The therapist wants to make fully informed decisions for successful diagnosis and resolution of the client's condition. How can an approach that limits access to the phenomena emerge and acquire strong support in clinical practice? The answer to this puzzle lies in part in the very nature of consciousness.

Consciousness is structuring in nature, and whatever is present to it becomes an object *for* it. The thrust of intentional thought delineates the phenomena as much as possible for conceptualization and reflective thought. We recognize and articulate our world as concepts give form to what we experience. The more sophisticated and refined our initially empirical concepts become the more we are able to develop more abstract concepts.

The process of being conscious of something is generally lost in the presence of the object. Typically, consciousness carries no sense of itself into its own activities. It is not *thematic*. In this way consciousness is analogous to perception, and its structure is more easily understood with an example of the way in which perception works: "Let us imagine a black dot on a white surface. Looking at them, one sees them spatially together and at the same time; and when one concentrates on the black dot, the white surface is relegated to the periphery of the visual field" (Shmueli 1971, 108).

Ordinarily, perception is unaware of itself. We see something and are aware of *that thing*. To try to think about the activity of perception loses its immediacy, as well as misses the immediacy of *that* reflecting: "When attention is focussed to the white surface, the dot recedes to the periphery" (Shmueli 1971, 108). In like manner, consciousness can focus on its object or on itself, but it can never wholly objectify itself: "One reflects and reflects upon one's reflections, but there must always be a reflecting, naming consciousness that can never be cornered and named by anyone" (Wilshire 1982, 227). To be conscious of something is to presuppose limits on the intentional structure that cannot be questioned, because to be conscious of consciousness itself requires a structure for intentionality. Thus, reflection on the world turns everything into *results for consciousness*; our notions of reality are often tied in strongly with that about which we are directly aware. Indeed, it is difficult to be aware of anything that has *not* been thus brought before consciousness for direct apprehension and verbal expression. That which we can think about in articulate, linguistic terms is clearly more accessible than the subjective background that allows us to think at all, and it is thus more practically manageable for comprehension and articulation.

The self-limiting nature of consciousness gives us an important clue for understanding strong preferences for objectivity. Since that about which we are conscious is an object of consciousness, our attention is most naturally focused objectively, that is, we pay little or no heed to the structure of conscious experiencing. The *content* of consciousness is so strongly present that it appears to be the totality of that which I *can* be aware. I see the chair; I don't think about the background that makes it a focal point for me. The convenience and clarity of the products of consciousness effectively block us from exploring other avenues for the development of knowledge.

Once objects achieve such status, the move is made in theories of knowledge to reorient language to depict only that which is commensurable with objective facts. A parallel move is made in therapies that rely on such theoretical biases. What we talk about must be objectively verifiable, and what we know must be directly expressible in language. The very tool with which we articulate objective reality is employed to serve a specific bias about reality. The possibilities for finding language to be deficient as a "reality-delineator" are severely reduced. Rather than allowing a dialectic between what we can say and what we experience, we simply reduce reality to language. Objective conventions are then generated for the professional community to follow, and those who are subsequently trained under the conventions support, often unwittingly, the bias. (There is currently a mood, passed on to students, among psychologists to avoid philosophical inquiry into basic concepts). Standards are set to ensure exclusive focus on objective content, and the term "objective" evolves from a basic *reference* to objects of consciousness to a *prescribed stance* of attending to them. *How* we perceive or experience this "what" is ultimately ignored. The experienc*ed*, linguistically captured, obscures then cuts off the flow of experienc*ing*.

How philosophical objectivist error has historically influenced therapy will be dealt with in the following section, beginning with

Freud. A sampling of therapeutic approaches from a wide variety of philosophical orientations should adequately illustrate the impact on clinicians of the subtle bias of "scientific psychology" in filtering human experiencing into "objective data."

The Objective Bias: Its Influence on Clinical Theory

The scientific community emphasizes knowledge that will stand up by itself. Objective approaches appear to offer a way to gain such knowledge. Whatever is free of the influences of a human subject *must* be able to stand up without a human knower. Psychology aligns itself with this bias, viewing itself as a part of the scientific community, and "objectivity" dominates theory and practice, sometimes even among those who tolerate the notion of subjectivity as an influence in our thinking.

Psychotherapy relies on a rationale for its methods and is thus prone to the influence of theoretical foundations that are developed under the auspices of scientific objectivity. Assumptions made about the human personality are formulated according to worldviews that grow out of the objective bias, and therapists who rely on these assumptions are subtly drawn into a reduction of their spectrum of awareness.

The therapist desires to exercise maximum jurisdiction over the details of the clinical situation. The results of objectivity in the natural sciences are attractive. Control and systematic packaging appear to be offered with an objective approach. However, "objectivity" is interpretable in a variety of ways, as is evident from the many different types of theories developed and used by clinical practitioners. A brief survey of several prominent clinical theories reveals the broad spectrum of possibilities for utilizing objectivity in therapeutic interaction. We can see from this survey that "objectivity" is a human construct and, as such, it can be shown to be but one possible perspective—a perspective that may not allow clinicians to do all they could do with and for their clients.

Sigmund Freud adhered to the Zeitgeist created by nineteenth-century scientists and historians who believed that "facts" were observable, verifiable entities; "facts" spoke for themselves, and all the gatherable "facts" constituted a "mirror" of the "truth." The observer and recorder of truth was to be "objective" in order to "amass all the hard facts required for a precise account of what really happened" (Geha 1983, 30) to facilitate the establishment of universal laws.

Freud hoped to proceed in such a manner, to accurately retell the evidence of the facts as it was told to him. His original seduction theory was just such an attempt to replicate and organize the data of factual occurrences. According to this theory, the outbreak of pathology was produced by an actual event of sexual seduction in the patient's past. Grounded in the Newtonian materialist tradition, Freud postulated unconscious memory traces as historical documents of these past factual situations. However, when it was revealed that many of the seduction accounts had been imagined, the theory fell apart.

Freud was shocked, feeling that reality as he believed it to be had slipped through his fingers:

> When this aetiology broke down under the weight of its own improbability and contradiction in definitely ascertainable circumstances, the result at first was helpless bewilderment. . . . The firm ground of reality was gone. . . . The new fact which emerges is precisely that they [the hysterical subjects] create such scenes in fantasy, and this psychical reality requires to be taken into account alongside practical reality. ([1914] 1957, 17–18)

Yet, despite his initial failure, Freud retained his materialist outlook and attempted to redefine reality as psychical fact:

> When I had pulled myself together, I was able to draw the right conclusions from my discovery: namely that the neurotic symptoms were not related directly to actual events but to phantasies embodying wishes, and that as far as the neurosis was concerned, psychical reality was more important than material reality. ([1925] 1959, 3)

Although this comment appears to be a move away from materialism, in reality the "phantasies" were still perceived by Freud to be wrapped around some historical truth. In *Moses and Monotheism*, he indicates that historical truth has its roots in material truth.

Swiss psychiatrist Ludwig Binswanger points out that Freud reduced all human life history to natural history, a reduction that does little justice to human existence:

> Freud approaches man with the idea of the natural man, the 'homo natura'. According to this idea, which is possible only on the basis of a complete taking apart of being-human as such and a natural-scientific-biological reconstruction of it, psychoanalysis has developed its entire critique and interpretation of the historical experiential material. (1958, 314)

He believes Freud's approach transforms human possibility into genetic developmental processes, turning human beings into "drive-dominated" creatures. The person is "lost in the theoretical scheme of an 'apparatus' of psychic mechanisms" (315).

Paul Ricouer (1970) describes Freud's allegiance to material realism as a deeply ingrained conviction that was retained, despite its initial failure, as the basis of truth. Referring to Freud's short paper "Formulations of the Two Principles of Mental Functioning" from 1911, Ricouer claims:

> He [Freud] was able to tie his truth principles in psychoanalysis to that of reality inasmuch as the real is . . . the ultimate horizon beyond the death of the fantasy. . . . Freud never relinquished the stubborn conviction that the fantasy stood out against the background of a primordial contact with an undeceptive reality. . . . It was on the basis of this concept of reality that Freud felt he was able to maintain the continuity between psychoanalysis and the sciences of physical and biological reality. (252)

The "evidence" of this reality, however, was ambiguous, requiring extensive interpretation to bring it into the fold of the theory.

It is evident to most readers of Freud that his mechanist and determinist fidelities deeply influenced and shaped his theoretical orientations with regard to the human psyche, even to the point of extreme personal defensiveness (Becker 1974); his development of psychopathological categories and constructs were consequently of an objectivist nature. He saw the world through a viewpoint that represented human beings as complex creatures whose nature could be broken down into simpler material (and thus observable) elements and analyzed as factual data.

Many modern analysts of the Freudian tradition maintain the integrity of Freud's theoretical constructs, utilizing the entire system of neurotic and psychotic complexes, causally determined mechanisms, developmental stages, and so forth. Karl Menninger (1958), a well-known analytic practitioner, confirms this:

> The patient is always communicating something. . . . The burden is on the analyst to discover what conflicts, impulses, defenses, resistances, attitudes, themes, etc., the patient is expressing via these various verbal and non-verbal forms of communication. This attitude helps the analyst to remain the ally of the patient's ego as it struggles with the id. (12)

This systematic orientation dictates the perceptions and interpretations of the analyst, fixing an *a priori* framework of stable concepts that objectify the patient through his or her presenting symptoms. The terms that were originally meant to explore human territory have assumed specific referential meaning by being associated in an explanatory structure; initially no more than tools to aid in a conceptual grasp of vague phenomena, they have become dogma—a way of casting the illusion of control over aspects of human experience. *What* a person is to the analyst is labeled and placed in a context that is abstracted from actual human existence.

The "cognitive-dynamic" theories moved away from traditional analytic approaches but retained a strongly objective orientation in theory and in clinical procedure. Relying on the patient's ability to mobilize rational processes for overcoming emotional difficulties, these theory builders developed constructs to stabilize what the patient is experiencing. Reality Therapy is an example.

In the late 1960s and early 1970s, William Glasser (1965) designed Reality Therapy on the basis of the belief that an individual's behavior could be viewed against an objective standard of measure: "reality." Each person, according to this theory, functions in harmony or disharmony with reality as he or she strives to satisfy a basic need for identity and self-respect:

> To be worthwhile, we must maintain a satisfactory standard of behavior. To do so, we must learn to correct ourselves when we do wrong and to credit ourselves when we do right. If we do not evaluate our behavior, or having evaluated it, we do not act to improve our conduct where it is below our standards, we will not fulfill our need to be worthwhile and we will suffer. (10)

The clients' behavior patterns are generated by their manner of striving for a sense of themselves as worthwhile persons. Objective standards (typically derived from how the therapist views "reality") determine whether such patterns are wrong or right. *What* the behavior is draws the focus of the therapist as it is compared to the standard for correct behavior. The experiencing of the person behaving is not a relevant factor. The individual has *a need* and thus *behaves* in some way to meet that need. Neither the therapist's nor the client's subjective sense of the situation is noted, except insofar as that "sense" can be distilled into objective behavioral and psychical constructs that constitute the dynamics of the theory. Glasser interpreted what he observed according to a set of ideas and came up with an objective system of therapeutic analysis that was unlike the objective orientation of the psychoanalysts.

Rational-Emotive Therapy, a creation of Albert Ellis, is another example of cognitive-dynamic therapies. According to Ellis, patho-logical symptoms are products of social learning: people strongly retain dysfunctional or maladaptive ideas because of learning pro-cesses. Emotional and intellectual processes are viewed as so closely tied together that the therapist purportedly has access to experienc-ing through what the client thinks about:

> Thinking and emotion are closely inter-related and at times differ mainly in that thinking is more tranquil, less somatically involved. . . . Since man is a uniquely sign-, symbol-, and language-creating animal, both thinking and emotions tend to take the form of self-talk or internalized sentences; and . . . the sentences that human beings keep telling them-selves are or become their thoughts or emotions. (1958, 36)

If a therapist can just get an individual to communicate his or her "self-talk," the therapist can correct the source of the person's emo-tional difficulties. Ellis maintains that people have the capacity to be rational, but irrational beliefs often influence their behavior. If rational thinking is maximized and irrational thinking minimized, all psychological disturbances can be corrected (1962). Ellis has syste-matically drawn up lists of the most common irrational beliefs so that therapists can simply look at the list, figure out which one is held by their client, and set about correcting such thinking. What clients tell themselves is what they are experiencing, Ellis claims, and individual experiencing can be generalized through typical pat-terns of "self-talk." Thus, the fullness of an individual's encounter with the world is construed as objectively accessible to, and directly expressible for, therapeutic scrutiny and diagnosis.

Along with generalization, systematic thoroughness is a goal of the objective approach. Such is the force behind George Kelly's Personal Construct Therapy. Kelly believes that the way in which people interpret some aspects of their personal worlds will deter-mine what and how they perceive, remember, learn, think, and be-have. He formulates a series of constructs with which he attempts to organize the modes of these interpretations. Some constructs are then shown to be more adaptive than others, and therapy helps clients find this out and to reconstrue their lives in accord with the adaptive constructs.

Each construct has formal characteristics by which it is catego-rized and organized into a systematic hierarchy. This approach is viewed by Kelly as patterned on natural scientific procedures. He strives to bring personal orientations to public view by means of their shared general features: "we attempt to piece together this high-level type of data [personalized constructs] with what we know about other persons" (1955, 455). These general patterns subsume individual experiencing so that the therapist can ignore everything not mediated through the constructs. The entire enterprise is so complex and so highly organized that it at least appears to be, according to the professional community, exhaustive of everything necessary for a comprehensive account of human existence. The constructs are objectively construed and the therapy can remain completely on objective terms.

"Objectivity" can also be understood in physicalist terms. Some therapists focus exclusively on biological processes. For example, both Megavitamin Therapy and Biocentric Therapy rely on the manipulation of objectively detectable biochemical processes (such as through a change in diet or with a drug) to bring about changes in the personality and/or behavior of the client (Herink 1980). These processes are publicly accessible with the proper instruments and are observed, measured, and recorded through statistical analysis. What "ails" the client is easily objectified, and since diagnosis and treatment consist exclusively of observation and manipulation of these physical processes, the client's subjectivity is completely irrelevant in the procedure.

The most extreme emphasis on objectivity comes from behaviorist circles. The influence of empiricist philosophies such as logical positivism is strong (Collingwood 1951; Hempel 1959; E. Nagel 1961). States of affairs are stripped of anything not objectively verifiable and open to public access (that is, access through explanation and linguistic communication). The clinician is expected to come up with precise, repeatable, and generalizable products. Even the language of this approach is restricted to technical terms with unambiguous referential functions, analogous to the principles of formal logic. Observation thus proves to be an essential tool for objectifying and verifying that which is utilized in therapy. Indirect observational bearing is allowed only through appropriate logical links to already warranted statements. Without a means for public verification, there is no good reason for holding any statement about human phenomena as either true or meaningful. The therapist is required to aspire to a perspectiveless vantage point in order to utilize properly the tools of logic and science.

Behavioral therapies form a body of related approaches: classical conditioning, Systematic Desensitization, Implosive Therapy, Modeling, and operant conditioning. These therapies are bonded by a common doctrine that describes learning and emotional difficulties as treatable through prescriptive, mechanical procedures.

As Andrew Salter (1964), a behavioral therapist, put it: "We are therapists—mechanics, if you please—and the theory we want is the theory that leads us to what to do to change the material we work with" (23). The focus is strictly on external determinants:

> Let us consider the conditioning therapies. These methods stem from the conception that neuroses are persistent, unadaptive habits that have been conditioned. . . .
> The fundamental overcoming of a neurosis *can* consist of nothing but deconditioning or undoing the relevant habit patterns. (Wolpe 1964, 8)

Nothing but behavioral patterns is recognized as therapeutically relevant, and the ideal procedure in therapy is to objectify everything that is admitted into the therapeutic arena:

> The concepts with which we direct the patient's activity and the concepts by which we approach the patient's material are all objective. Let us remember that just as Pavlov could count the number of drops of saliva secreted by a parotid gland in a dog, we can study the "secretions" of the human brain, coming out of the patient's mouth in the form of words. (Salter 1964, 23)

A behaviorist views all clinical phenomena as learned or conditioned verbal, emotional, or motor responses that are maintained and manipulated by reinforcement/punishment schedules: "In describing the behavior called neurotic as learned, the emphasis is on indicating that this behavior is initially the result of various external operations such as reinforcement, generalization, and contiguity . . ." (Reyna 1964, 171).

The idea is that behavioral data are "accurate" data and nothing else is quite as accurate; accuracy is the goal and measurement is the method: "Any qualitative report is a quantity of something" (Salter 1964, 23). The behavioral therapist aims to objectify human existence into publicly verifiable products and then to recast these products by means of theoretical interpretation and physiological science into quantitatively measurable items. Therapy, then, is basically a one-sided affair between an observer and an observee. This approach is the ultimate form of objectivism, eschewing everything but that which can be objectified. The only features of human phenomena that are certified *as* phenomena are those that are observable such that the client is no more than an object to the therapist's view. Any reference to inner processes that are not behaviorally manifested is meaningless.

The behaviorist has interpreted "objectivity" as quite a narrow and restrictive term. An "object" is no more than that which is externally observable. Yet such restrictions misconstrue "internal" data as "subjective." That is, a behaviorist would view an introspective account as "subjective" because it is not externally accessible. Yet that which is produced through introspection is also an object for consciousness and is thus as "objective" as behavior.

Therapies that rely on introspection reduce experiencing to "inwardly" grasped experience. The introspective question is "What do you experience?" or "What do you inwardly perceive?" Immediate experiencing is reconstrued as "data" that are observable with the "mind's eye." The "subjective" is viewed as an internal substance that can be sorted out with the proper methods and with disciplined concentration. The misunderstanding of treating objective data as if they were subjective further aggravates the lack of awareness of subjectivity as the "how" of experiencing; the non-objectifiable experiencing that is background to, and feeds into, the objectifying process is ignored. Subjectivity is not caught in its immediacy by introspection. The focus is on the content of the conscious processes as objects for consciousness.

The "father" of introspectionism, Wilhelm Wundt, attempted to break down elements of consciousness by utilizing methods from physiology. Self-observation was experimentally controlled—a skill developed only through a rigorous apprenticeship. Controlled manipulation and repeatability were essential features of this procedure. The elements of consciousness were thus determined to be sensations and feelings, both of which were classifiable on continuums of quantity and quality: sensations were measured for modality, intensity, and duration; and feelings ranged on a three-dimensional scale from agreeable to disagreeable, from tension to relaxation, and from excitement to depression (Schultz 1975). It should be clear from this account that what is generally regarded as a subjectively oriented exercise is as objective as any other approach that focuses on objects of consciousness *as* objects.

Yet even therapies that note the impact of and strive to include subjectivity as an essential part of therapy often fall into objective systemizing, sometimes even to the point of threatening to exclude the experiencing of the client. Representing this family of therapies is Ludwig Binswanger (1956), included in Rollo May's *Existence* as an example of a therapist who designs his theories with a deep appreciation for the subjective experiencing of his clients. Binswanger bases his therapeutic procedures on Martin Heidegger's descriptions of self and "being-in-the-world"—the modes of human existence. Binswanger's basic tenet is that each individual has a set of personal "meaning matrixes," or a "world-design"—objectively construed categories:

> Whenever we speak of forms of existence, we are speaking of forms of being-in-the-world. . . . Structurally these forms refer to the forms of the world. Indeed, it is *in* the world that an actual existence "lives". Hence these forms are "being-in" any given world, and refer to the self which corresponds to this being-in. . . . (23)

The meaning matrix makes up the world according to an individual's perspective, filtered through personal descriptive categories; it can be enlarged with new experiences or rigidified when threatened by them. Binswanger explores what the client says or acts out— whatever means are used for expression—and he uses these expressions to map out common denominators of meaning for that person. He feels that he acknowledges subjective experiencing in this manner.

However, although Binswanger struggles with the bias, he is somewhat prone to focusing on objectively accessible constructs of a person's mode of being. As Burstow (1980) points out, Binswanger relies so strongly on constructs that he, too, becomes reductionistic:

> The most frequent scenario is: there is only one or two constructs in the person's matrix. The person has an experience which clashes with one of them. The person experiences trauma, that is, he experiences his world as threatened. He frantically tries to safeguard the threatened category. . . . (245)

That is, Binswanger appears to draw individual cases into a generalized theory of personality and then approach other cases with this theory intact, instead of allowing these other cases to retain their own individuality. Although each person's meaning matrix is purportedly regarded as unique and informative of that individual's subjectivity, the bulk of the therapeutic work is done through a generalized schema, in objective terms. Human possibilities not in accord with this framework are almost as vulnerable to being reframed or obscured and ignored as they are with the other theories mentioned.

While this list of types of therapies is not intended to be exhaustive—Herink (1980) listed more than two hundred and fifty different approaches to therapy—it does reveal the thread of bias running through the professional clinical community. Some therapies are more oriented than others toward systematic categorization and control, but insofar as any approach obscures or neglects the subjective flow of experiencing in the therapeutic situation, it is guilty of partializing and fragmenting the world of the client.

Objectivity and Objectivism

Both "objective" and "subjective" approaches to therapy entail some degree of objectivity in that both utilize the intentional operations of consciousness that issue in objects *for* consciousness. For the behaviorists, the object is behavior; for Ellis, it is "self talk;" for Binswanger, it is the personal world "matrix." Articulation and expression are hardly possible without this activity, and theories depend on language for construction, analysis, critique, and communication. Objectivity *qua* objectivity is hardly a negative quality. To understand or to communicate anything requires some objective means: we make sense of our world to ourselves and to others through objective concepts. Clients can give therapists a better initial grasp of the central issues or problems if they can say a few things about their circumstances and feelings.

However, the automatic process of objectifying the world for the purposes of communication can generate the belief that the world is given to us, in its totality, by means of—and *only* of—this process. This is objectivism, as outlined earlier. To repeat, reality is defined as exhaustively accessible to objective methods of discovery and interpretation: all states of affairs are knowable and directly expressible through objective, linguistic concepts. This belief cuts off the discovery and apprehension—and therapuetic utilization!—of aspects of human engagements that are not caught up in propositions. While *objectivity* as a conscious process allows reality to consist of more than the objective, *objectivism* does not. The difference between these two concepts can be seen in the contrast between therapies that adopt the respective concepts.

Binswanger uses objective categories for his conceptual framework, but derives these categories from the integration of both objective and nonobjectifiable phenomena:

> Since "world" always means not only the What within which an existence exists but at the same time the How and Who of its existing, the forms of the How and Who, of the Being-in and Being-oneself, become manifest quite "of their own accord" from the characterization of the momentary world. (1958, 269)

Binswanger believes the "world-design" of the client furnishes information about the "how" as well as about the "what": the "how" is acknowledged by the therapist in virtue of his or her own humanity: "It still depends on the imagination of the single researcher . . . how truly he is able to re-experience and resuffer, by virtue of his own existential abilities . . ." (1958, 209). The therapist is encouraged to remain aware of how he or she intrudes on interpretation and procedure. Not all of the structures of experience that generate language about experience are themselves objectifiable, yet they may be present to some degree in the objective description. Since Binswanger acknowledges both objective and subjective phenomena, he manages to be objective without being objectivist.

Behavioral therapies, on the other hand, focus entirely on the objects of external observation; that which can be observed from an external viewpoint and verified by other external observers comprises human reality. Human beings are perceived as a class of objects among other classes of objects in the material world and, consequently, as approachable through exclusively objective means, such as observation, for gaining information. "Objectivity" in this approach is a prescription for total objectivism: everything that *is* is objectifiable for qualified third persons.

It might appear to follow that, if the natural objectification of consciousness is both a positive and a necessary means of gaining and adding to our store of knowledge about human existence, the more "objective" one is, the more knowledge one can gain. In addition, the more the knowledge gained can be verified by others, the freer it will be of individual points of view; and the freer it is of such influence, the more secure it will be as knowledge. This is the opinion of the objectivist (e.g., logical positivism). It assumes that nothing comprises knowledge but that which is objectively attainable. While such logic makes good sense on the level of definitions and logical implication, the extremes of objectivism push human inquirers into prejudices that, in actual practice, are limiting and restrictive.

In therapeutic literature, the difference between an objectivity cognizant of the lived background world of the client—the excess dough outside the cookie cutter of *what* is said—and an objectivism that takes the cookies and ignores the scraps can be seen when reading accounts of actual cases. In simple descriptions of behavior or physical processes or "constructs," the client seems lost, distanced. We know Anna O. through her symptoms. Clients are more humanly accessible if actual transcripts of conversations are available. We can see for ourselves the contradictions, the stutterings, the uncertainties, the self-blindness, the helplessness. Yet even in transcripts, something of the client is lost to us. We fail to see subtle changes in posture, tiny lines of resistance forming at the eyes, unexpressed fear. Most of all, we have no access to the lived experience of being in the same room with the client, of sensing that which cannot be adequately brought to light in description. As Kierkegaard ([1846] 1968) put it: "knowledge has a relationship to the knower, who is essentially an existing individual, and for this reason, all essential knowledge is essentially related to existence" (177).

In accounts of human existence where objectivism dominates, human experiencing is in large part ignored or cut away. Therapies that subscribe to this perspective strain communication between client and therapist through pragmatic membranes that result from pressure to gain control, accuracy, and verification. The professional is trained toward conceptualization of *the experienced*, viewing that which is conceptualized as the total content of human experiencing rather than as a possibly distorting *mediation* of experiencing for the purposes of expression and classification. Appropriating such a bias unreflectively, then teaching it to others as "the way," generates an automatic belief in the tenets of that bias, one of which is that *no bias distorts the phenomena*. The perspective is presented as nonperspectival—the product of human thought having none of the trappings of human activity that make thinking possible. Therapy channeled through such a bias is prone to its extremes: human thought is detached from a human thinker and the exploration of human existence is done by an existing human being who purportedly stands outside of human existence.

The Self-Deception of Objectivism

Logically ordered knowledge, purified of individual distortion, is viewed as not only highly desirable but strongly credible, and it becomes a priority in therapy when it offers a sense of control and a means of avoiding ambiguous and indeterminate aspects of the phenomenal flux. Objectifiable entities are made genei ¹ and absolute through categorization, so that therapeutic attention can be selectively focused on those features of the phenomena that are prominent to an objectifying consciousness.

This approach presents itself to the clinical practitioner as an accurate and definitive means by which to assess reality in total; the objective bias is not recognized *as* a bias because the apparent ease of objectivist access to "all of reality" *eclipses the act of defining reality in exclusively objective terms.* When one believes that one has all the tools necessary to pin down reality, why look any further? The question of reality is begged at the very foundation of such a belief, but this fact is easily dismissed by compiling more and more data. The objectivist assumption is blurred in the act of defining reality and then erased in the definition, roughly as history is effectively erased in chauvinist countries when facts, events, and people are blotted out to suit the ideology. The therapist struggling to assess human conditions and to produce results that will justify the effort is easily seduced by the desire for accuracy, closure, and control into adopting the objectivist bias.

Objectivism develops into an approach that is close to what Daniel Dennett (1978) calls "loans of intelligence." He contends that theory building involves such loans because endowing anything in a system with content intelligible in that system posits something that understands that content. The "loan" is repaid by analyzing away the comprehender. Otherwise rationality would be taken for granted. For example, a strict theory of behaviorism requires, first, a theoretician who is not prone to reinforcement schedules that might show the theory itself to be merely a matter of environmental influences. He must stand outside the system in order to describe it. Then he must be dismissed. That is, the abstract thinker who posits a theory about human existence assumes a human being who understands the theory; but then the thinker is defined as nonessential in the theory itself.

However, despite the available means by which thinkers can escape themselves, therapists will still be confronted with facets of their clients that defy or elude general explanations and descriptions. When a client describes a vivid and upsetting dream, the therapist can record the words used and the behavior manifested during the description, but cannot fully depict the lived experiencing of the client as the dream unfolds in a public manner. Nor does the therapist have full access to the qualitative structure of the impact of the dream itself on the client. However much the client might say, there is a significant difference between the words used and the experiential effects of the dream. Objective theory has yet to solve the problem of its own mediation; nor has it been able to fully objectify the immediacies of acts of consciousness—the raw experiencing involved in the very attempts to reflect on experiencing. General concepts are inherently detached from the particularities of an experiencing individual and can, at best, only vaguely reflect the life of that individual. Rollo May (1958) views this as a genuine impotence:

How can we be certain that our system, admirable and beautifully wrought as it may be in principle, has anything whatever to do with this specific Mr. Jones, a living immediate reality sitting opposite us in the consulting room? . . . How can we know whether we are seeing the patient in his real world . . . which is for him unique, concrete and different from our general theories of culture? (35)

Thomas Nagel (1979) echoes this concern:

If the subjective nature of experiencing is fully comprehensible only from one point of view, then any shift to greater objectivity—that is, less attachment to a specific viewpoint—does not take us nearer to the real nature of the phenomena: it takes us farther away from it. (174)

That is, a theoretical context for the person might be nothing short of an abrogation rather than a revelation of personal, concrete human existence. Explanation in terms of generalities does not seem to do justice to an individual's life as it is lived.

Such an impasse threatens the claims of objectivism both as a comprehensible means of discovery and as an adequate theory of knowledge. Some theoretical moves can be and sometimes are made to advance an illusion that nothing of a troublesome nature has been encountered. To try to avoid or ignore subjective phenomena can take one of several directions. Thomas Nagel lists them as reduction, elimination, and annexation (1979, 210).

The reduction of subjectivity to objective terms is a contradiction, since there is no literal linguistic expression for that which eludes reference. The attempt produces an artificial language that fails to capture what it purports to capture. The resulting form is public and general, but the private specifics are still excluded. For example, to define aspects of individual experiencing in terms of behavioral constructs is to deal only with the behavioral elements and to define out of existence, theoretically, everything else. It is also to fit individuals into an anonymous schema such that individual features become irrelevant. Yet using a theory to define something as nonexistent or irrelevant will not account for it. Such a practice amounts to nothing short of deferring to a theory because one *wants* it to be true rather than because it *is* true. It begs the question by assuming that no proof of the theory is needed. This approach is much like the replacement of the English language in George Orwell's *1984* with "Newspeak," a language designed to prevent the expression or even the act of thinking of any ideas not sanctioned by "the Party." A second pitfall of reduction is that objectification of subjective phenomena transforms everything into content—a "what"—while the "how" remains untouched. Reduction as a defense of objectivism is inadequate and does not resolve the difficulty of subjectivity; it only appears to do so superficially.

Elimination amounts to dismissing nonverbalizable subjectivity as nothing more than an illusion. Gilbert Ryle takes this action in *The Concept of Mind* (1966). He addresses the purported problem of the inability to know about the act of knowing *as* the act takes place. Although it is perhaps true, he admits, that acts of knowledge cannot be sweepingly exhaustive, that which is left out in any given moment is not privileged to escape forever. It could be the target of the very next act of knowledge. In principle everything is knowable, according to Ryle. Objective knowledge is sufficient knowledge. That which appears to be elusive is not. It will either be hit accurately by the ensuing moment's act of knowledge, or else there is no substance to it and it can be dismissed. This is another patent begging of the question, relying on a circular definition of objectivity and reality: reality is objectively knowable, and whatever is not knowable is not real. Such circular thinking prevents any real attempt to deal with the issue of subjectivity. Indeed, Ryle can hardly make a definitive claim about the "unreflected moment" because neither he nor anyone else can know *what* that moment actually entails. We cannot even say with certainty that it eludes us, but the clinical data point more strongly to the latter possibility than to Ryle's confident assertion. Even "reflective" persons experience blindspots. And even in those cases where reflection *could* supply accurate propositional knowledge of immediate qualities of experiencing, it can never supply the *feeling* of the experiencing; the ultimate irony is that too much analytic reflection can go so far as to *prevent* us from feeling the very qualities about which we are being propositionally accurate. Reflection cannot be described with certainty as thoroughly self-illuminating since we cannot reflect on the actual moment of reflecting; rather, the evidence from the manner in which persons are involved in the world indicates something different—that reflection can block us from lived awareness of the immediate qualities of our engagements. If consciousness were exhaustively self-illuminating, as Ryle (and Descartes) indicates, we would expect people to be much more aware of, and in control of, their own behavior.

Finally, inventing new elements of objective reality—annexation—is metaphysically messy and implausible. Like Plato's introduction of two realms of reality to allow for both change and permanence, adding things on is contrary to the objective goals of simplicity and unity in explanation. It is just such goals that provide the impetus for reduction and elimination. In the interest of truth, annexation cannot simply be dismissed out of desire for aesthetic purity, but where other options are available to accomplish the same or more productive ends, annexation seems an alternative worth side-stepping.

Each of these directions is nothing short of a failure to face the problem of subjectivity squarely. Subjective experiencing is partially or entirely neglected because the desire to view it as unimportant or unnecessary (or nonexistent!) to accounts of reality is already present in a perception of it that is biased by objectivism. If a person only looks for reality in the shape of enclosed squares, it is difficult to introduce circles or triangles to that individual's perception.

Despite the objectivist move toward general perspectives, the objective knower, as a human being, has an inherently particular perspective. Such people inevitably participate in both subjective and objective engagements with the phenomena of human existence. They experience the particularities of their own existence, although they try to reframe them in the intentional scope of a general, objectifying consciousness. The goal is to engulf themselves so much with abstraction and theoretical schemata that they are unaware of their subjectivity, and then to take the further step that blocks them from seeing that *they* have brought about this self-obscuring. Thus they can be easily convinced of the "obvious" objectivity of the phenomena.

R. H. Johnson (1972) describes this development away from individual viewpoints within the scientific community. He indicates that the limitations of an individual scientist's perspective inspire scientists to merge their points of view with those of other members of the profession. As a part of the community, a scientist can take on the perspective of the community that devotes itself to total and complete understanding of the world. The community is an entity in itself that possesses total and unlimited vision where everything fits into place. The scientist takes on this perspective as his or her own: "an individual becomes so used to strutting around in the vestments of the community that he forgets that these are not his own personal wardrobe" (42). Engulfment in the community dulls one's awareness of one's self as possessing a limited perspective. All questions are related to the community's attempt to advance knowledge. Contact with human life is made only through the intelligibility of general concepts. The scientist can know what something is but does not experience it:

When an individual becomes a philosopher or a scientist, he becomes a member of a community; he assumes the community's mode of existence. He learns to look at things through the eyes of the community and to speak with its voice. But if an individual becomes so accustomed to the community's mode of existence that he begins to think of its properties as his own; if he loses sight of the fact that his own existence is characterized by a sharply different set of properties, then he has begun to forget what it means to exist as a human being. (143)

How is such self-forgetting possible?

A person in pursuit of knowledge that will be credible to a community of other inquirers is influenced by the goals and methods of that community. Objective knowledge is held in high esteem and subjective influence is regarded as suspect. The goals of science echo Hegel's prescription: "the share of the total work of mind that falls to the activity of any particular individual can only be very small. Because this is so, the individual must all the more forget himself, as in fact the very nature of science implies and requires that he should . . ." (1964, 130).

Using an account of self-deception that is based on that described by Herbert Fingarette (1969), we can extrapolate insights from psychology to other areas of human endeavor. Individuals involved in the scientific community gradually make their objective engagements more and more explicit to themselves. As they reformulate their orientation to the world they take less account of subjective connections to their *experiencing* of their orientation. They fail to see that *what* they think has roots in their lived experiencing. The inarticulate immediacies of the individual's attempts to grasp phenomena, e.g., another person's experiential modes, are absorbed and shut out without that individual being aware of it. The therapist bent on collecting data or reinforcing theory will ignore and thus obscure the effects of his or her own subjective influences in the clinical situation. Gaps created in the objectivist stance by the penetration of subjectivity are shrugged off as the investigator's rationale for supporting objective engagements gains strength. The investigator sees how well the objective method applies to gathering information about objects in the world and easily extrapolates the approach to the study of human beings. It suits the purposes to make only the objective explicit.

That such people are *not* making their subjective engagements explicit is also not made explicit to themselves and they fall into a sort of absent-mindedness about this neglect. The more they rely on and make explicit their objective engagements, the more the integrity of the objective approach depends on the avoidance or implicit disavowal of subjective perspectives. Thus, "objective" investigators can live their subjective engagements without acknowledging them explicitly as their own, and without acknowledging that they have avoided them. Their manner of being persons is effectively isolated and relegated to a tacit dimension of their awareness, blurred and then eclipsed by an overt focus on purely objective engagements. They view their objective perspective as free of subjective distortion because they have lost an awareness of their own subjectivity.

Objections to the Objectivist Bias

It must be made clear at this point that not all verbal labeling of experience is a hindrance to therapy. There *are* times when a simple label can permeate a client's defenses effectively, as in the following case.

A sociology professor at a large university had experienced the suicide of his mother and the birth of his first child in the same week. He responded toward both events with an indifferent attitude that surprised his colleagues. He described both events as "natural life processes" and went on with his work. Within a few months, he sought therapy, complaining that he had begun to experience a block in his ability to relate to his students and to do his research.

The therapist perceived that the professor was angry at the interruption in his life of his mother's death and at the burden of responsibility of having an unplanned child. While in some situations the label "anger" might rip a neatly idealized abstraction out of the concrete flow of experience, in the case of the professor it provided a wedge with which the therapist was able to probe feelings obscured by layers of academic rationalizations.

Objectification can, at times, be an aid to therapy. The actual *use* of verbal labels is not at issue here; what is at issue is the attitude that such labels should be utilized *exclusively* in therapy. The therapist must learn the flexibility of deciding when labels are helpful and when they only obscure.

Therapists who are objectivists practice their profession at an expense to both themselves and their clients. They disregard the experiencing that makes a person's point of view unique in its particularities because such phenomena do not fit into their abstracted theoretical systems.

Søren Kierkegaard is famous for his attack on the systematic abstractions formulated by Hegel. He refers to the self-forgetful nature of such thinking not only as seriously incomplete for the sake of theory, but also as ludicrous:

The questionable character of abstract thought becomes apparent, especially in connection with all existential problems, where abstract thought
gets rid of the difficulty [of penetrating concrete reality] by leaving it out,
and then proceeds to boast of having explained everything. . . .

Such an abstract thinker, one who neglects to take into account the
relationship between his abstract thought and his own existence as an
individual, not careful to clarify his own relationship to himself, makes a
comical impression . . . because he is in the process of ceasing to be a
human being. ([1846] 1968, 267–68)

The abstract thinker deserts existence for the more alluring theoretical and methodological advantages of closed conceptual thought.

Kierkegaard goes on to claim that such a state of affairs is inevitable for the individual who strives for complete objectivity. The
fullness of human existence will not tolerate the separation of
thought from the thinker. However, pure objective thought cannot
prevent the separation:

Objective thinking is wholly indifferent to subjectivity and hence also to
inwardness and appropriation. . . . It is direct and lacks the elusiveness
and art of a double reflection [the sense of one's relation to one's own
thinking] . . . which belongs to subjective thinking. . . . Objective thinking is conscious only of itself. ([1846] 1968, 71)

In short, the investigator of human phenomena who strives for total
objectivity grows inevitably into a duplex being. Such people cannot
escape the particularities of their concrete and personal reality if
they want to continue as beings who can think, but they also want to
think thoughts that are purified of this personal existence.

George Atwood and Robert Stolorow (1984) expose the contradiction inherent in the desire to separate oneself from one's human
existence: "the investigator is an experiencing individual, situated
personally and historically, and his quest for knowledge is accordingly subject to the influence of all those historical, personal, and
circumstantial factors that come into play in every human action"
(3).

They then point out: "The notion that a single investigator can
disengage himself from involvement in the world and uncover
through his own isolated reflections the foundational structures of
experience implies a denial of human finiteness . . ." (13).

Scientists, points out C. Stephen Evans (1977), are not sometimes
scientists, sometimes persons. "Being a scientist is itself a form of
the personal, a way of being-in-the-world" (167). That is, abstraction implies a god's-eye-view and a belief that knowledge about hu-

man experience can be formulated outside of an experiential context. Pure thought abandons its relations to existence, much as a bridge is destroyed after the crossing. Under the auspices of objectivity, thought purports to articulate a mind-independent reality and then tries *to endow itself* with a mind-independent existence.

Therapists who try to practice such subject-independent thinking often find they have to involve themselves explicitly at some point in their abstractions. Freud reviewed each psychological clue as a fragmented reflection of reality but found that psychoanalysis could not gain all the facts, nor could it simply report them as they stood. He found that he had to invent "missing" facts in order to reconstruct an account of his patients that would make historic sense, coherent with a mechanist, materialist reality. His personal beliefs helped him fill in what was missing. A number of recent reviewers depict Freud's project as not so much a digging out of the actual historical facts but as a creative or "narrative" process in which he put together life stories of his patients that would be meaningful, coherent, and compelling. These reviewers point out that Freud relied on aesthetic and practical criteria (Geha 1984; Hillman 1975; Spence 1982; Weber 1982). Forced to use his imagination, Freud invariably infused his accounts with his own peculiar perspectives. No amount of methodological "unpacking" could make his case histories more accountable to the "facts." Too much "information" was improvization.

A "fact" is not isolatable from human conceptualization but is objectified as fact by some person, or by some community of persons. There may be a convincing rationale behind the "discernment" of given facts, but they are what they are and how they are because of some human conceptual activity. Modes of organization, Nelson Goodman (1978) points out, are not found in the world but are *built* into it. Organization and composition, weeding out and filling in, are "world-making" activities:

> If worlds are as much made as found, so also knowing is as much remaking as reporting. . . . Perceiving motion often consists in producing it. Discovering laws involves drafting them. Recognizing patterns is very much a matter of inventing and imposing them. Comprehension and creation go on together. (22)

Human thought is often directed by a desire to see things in a certain way, to make sense of the phenomena *for* human existence: "When desiring is primary for awareness, awareness is always structuring in nature and the structure of awareness will be meaning" (Scott

1982, 79). Variations in purpose will result in variations in "world-building."

The desire for objectively gained knowledge generates objective prescriptions and the belief that there *is* a perspectiveless vantage point such that a thing-in-itself will so appear to us. Yet the claim that this is possible arises within a worldview that is possible only with a human thinker.

Bertrand Russell (1959) points out that third-order knowledge is developed and carried on through already developed premises about perceived phenomena. "Knowledge by acquaintance," as he calls it, is direct, sensory knowledge, knowing nothing *about* the perceived. Second-order knowledge is knowledge about sensory awareness, while various levels of meaning are formulated in third-order knowledge. We react to the world according to our understanding of it, striving for explanation and unification of knowledge at the third level. We punctuate the flux of events to sort and evaluate them. Our definitions of reality, then, involve our own human relations to it.

Psychology is no exception to this, as Atwood and Stolorow (1984) point out: "psychoanalytic research is obviously not a philosophically neutral activity. It is based on premises about its subject matter and these premises guide and delimit the investigations it undertakes" (22). Giving some set of premises priority is a matter of a person's preferences, even if that person is subject to community censure.

Human involvement in knowledge about reality cannot be subtracted from that knowledge. Severing thought from existence raises problems with the veracity of accounts of existence that are supposedly drawn up without reference to the experience of the designer. Yet replacing the context of existence with abstract generalizations about existence is a sleight of hand that only fools those who so wish to be. Kierkegaard sums up this irony;

> If a man begins upon a parenthesis which becomes so long that he himself forgets that it is a parenthesis, this does not avail to cancel its parenthetical character; as soon as it is read in its context, it becomes manifest that to permit the parenthetical insertion to play the role of the main assertion is meaningless. ([1846] 1968, 298)

No person can entirely forget himself and still exist, in the fully human sense of the word, much less describe that existence in its fullness. To attempt to do so, says Deutscher (1983), does not serve objectivity but rather is irresponsible toward it, since true objectivity appears to be an intelligent, informed use of subjectivity, not an escape from it. Clear, uncluttered judgments *require* an accurate sense of ourselves as subjects, as people in a lived-world context. The involved self, in other words, is a *condition* of objectivity.

This concern with "the man" rather than with only the content of his observations and conceptualizations is often dismissed as *ad hominem* argumentation. However, the preceding discussion is not an "appeal to the man to support his ideas," nor is it an "attack on the man to discredit his ideas." Rather it is an attempt to retrieve the presence of the thinker in his thought and to show the impossibility of separation, especially with regard to human accounts about human existence. It does not seem too far-fetched to think that a person who describes what being a person is has utilized some sense of his or her own experiences *as* a person.

A broader criticism may also be leveled. Mistaking some feature in the genesis of a claim as a reason for regarding that claim as true or false is the genetic fallacy. Evidence for a logically correct argument consists of statements that, if true, provide reasons for accepting the argument as true. Referring to some psychological factor as a basis for either proposing or believing the argument is a mistake in reasoning; the psychological factor is not evidence for holding the argument to be true. For example, a frightening childhood experience could be part of the causal explanation for accepting a conclusion about the dangers of the dark, but it is not evidence. However, our proposal that a thinker is involved in his or her thinking is not this sort of mistaken reasoning. We are not proposing the thinker's relation to his or her thought as evidence for accepting the thought as true or false. We simply wish to show that thought without a thinker is not possible and, thus, thinking involves the thinker as a person who is in some way related to his or her thought.

Abstraction provides only one repository of meaning. Other possibilities lie in the specifics of personal existence, that is, the processes of human consciousness that defy conceptual stabilization and conventional verbal expression. Abstract categories are general idealities that can only elucidate dimensions of human existence as approximations. There is no perfect representation of lived actuality because there is no movement in concepts like there is in the existential processes that must be lived to be grasped. Individuals who live their existence have more concrete knowledge of themselves than any amount of general information can give them:

> Each individual has a knowledge of himself which is so intimate, so concrete, so immediate, and so kaleidoscopic that no author, not even the most skillful delineator of character can describe it.

. . . He always is in process, moving forward in time and in a sense coming into being every moment. (Anderson 1970, 206–7)

Existence *as actuality* separates thought and being, because to think that possibility (general thought) and actuality can be mediated without residue is to suppose that actuality can be subsumed totally under the categories of abstract thought. We must learn to live with the conceptually open-ended experiencing that brings about an un-resolvable dialectic of thought and being. Neither can subsume nor replace the other. Thought without a thinker is impossible and an existing being who is capable of thought but who refuses to think is a ridiculous figure. Objective thought must recognize its own bound-aries and allow subjectivity free play without trying to redefine it: "The difficulty that inheres in existence, with which the existing in-dividual is confronted, is one that never really comes to expression in the language of abstract thought" (Kierkegaard [1846] 1968, 267). An objectivized viewpoint cannot adequately address the problems of an existing individual.

The therapist who must deal with existing individuals seeks the best possible avenue for knowledge. Objectivism is the "path of least resistance" because a dialectical tension is difficult to maintain. Yet such an approach is an artifice of human beings, an attempt to make everything manageable. The psychologist Abraham Maslow (1966) describes this situation succinctly:

The search for a fundamental datum (in psychology) is itself a reflection of a whole world view, a scientific philosophy which assumes an atomis-tic world. . . .
    This artificial habit of abstraction, or working with reductive elements, has worked out so well and become so ingrained a habit that the abstrac-tors and reducers are apt to be amazed at anyone who denies the em-pirical or phenomenal validity of these habits. By smooth stages they convince themselves that this is the way in which the world is actually construed, and they find it easy to forget that, even though it is useful, it is still artificial . . . it is a man-made system that it imposed on an inter-connected world in flux. (38, 60)

Although the empirical standards of natural science can gain an aura of absolutism when science as a system forgets its systematizers, a more accurate sense of the standards would involve the dialectic of the conceptual and the conceptualizing. The standards are formu-lated by individuals who have an interest in them: "far from being neutral at heart, he [the scientist] is himself passionately interested in the outcome of the procedure. He must be, for otherwise he would never discover a problem at all and certainly not advance toward its solution" (Polanyi 1964, 34).

Applied to therapy, it follows that clinicians are interested in what they are doing, in the approach they take, and in the outcome of their procedures. Similarly, clients are interested in what they say to the therapist and in what they receive back. The involvement of the individual in his or her thinking requires an approach that will acknowledge this relation in its full interplay of lived actuality and general possibility.

Beyond Objectivism: Including Human Involvement

Subjectively oriented therapies develop from a recognition of the preceding concerns. This family of therapies shares common notions about the nature of persons. Therapy is viewed as an open-ended art, a continuous chain of improvizations clued into the unique particularities of individual clients. There is no automatic extrapolation from one client to another. The methods employed often result from a combination of the client's individuality and the therapist's sense of the client *as* an individual. A great deal of freedom is allowed in both the perception and diagnosis of the client's "presenting problems." Proponents of this approach include Ludwig Binswanger, Rollo May, Viktor Frankl, Medard Boss, Carl Rogers, and R. D. Laing.

While attunement to immediate experiencing is emphasized, there is some danger in the possibility of subjectivist exaggeration. Too much emphasis on individualism and points of view can lead to the dismissal of standards of any kind, making everything relative to the individual. An antiscientific attitude may be generated. Yet little can be gained for the professional dialectic if each and every case must be judged entirely by its own unique features (which would be impossible in any case). Patterns of human choice and action are detectable and even generalizable, although generalization should not be allowed to swallow up individuality. Neither objectivity nor subjectivity should dominate in the explanation of principles of human reality, but they should be viewed as complementary features of that reality that unfold together: "The key is recognizing that subjectivity and objectivity are not distinct realms of being. There is no such thing as 'pure' objectivity. . . . Subjectivity interpenetrates objectivity" (Evans 1983, 289). Inwardness is intentional; it always involves intentional objects and a world as lived, and it cannot be identified apart from that "content." Without the experiential ground there would be no such "content." When we treat the content as a self-subsisting thing-experienced, we abstract from the experiential ground and forget that we have done so. We become fantastic beings.

Therapists cannot be indifferent to existential factors, either in themselves or in their clients. If they view their clients as objects, the clients will come to view themselves as such and will fail to achieve the experiential immediacy necessary to decisions that involve them as a whole persons. The clinical phenomena must be allowed to be as they are, apart from *a priori* assumptions that could truncate them. Clients must be allowed to be both subject and object because their own existence involves a tension of the two modes of being: The individual is an object reflected in his or her reflecting as well as an experiencer involved in reflecting. Since counselling is meant to be a process by which clients can gain some coherent sense of themselves and of their manner of existing, the therapist must recognize that objective inquiry alone has limited application. Doing psychology cannot be merely a matter of assimilating a body of objective "facts" about human activity because no objectively constructed "mirror of reality" will succeed as a construction of total truth about human beings.

Thomas Nagel (1979) suggests that the only sensible action is to "resist the voracity of the objective appetite, and stop assuming that understanding of the world and our position in it can always be advanced by detaching from that position and subsuming whatever appears from there under a single, more comprehensive conception" (211). Some things can be acknowledged, perhaps, from no particular point of view—a "view from nowhere"—but not everything. Any account of the person that will have therapeutic meaning *for* a person must be construed in terms of directly lived significance, i.e., inclusive of subjectivity. The "facts" of human reality are inextricably embedded in human contexts of experiencing, meaning, and personal relevance.

Thought by a thinker bears a relation to that thinker; existence gives to the thinker particular times, places, and experiences. Existence is the intersection of actuality and ideality. Our task is to make the intersection negotiable, livable. The self that is interested in its own existence is not the Cartesian or Kantian "subject," an abstract and empty dynamic center for an objective system; it is a concrete person, existing in the fullness of his or her own experiencing. Such a self is not objectifiable from either a first- or third-person point of view. Thus, neither the therapist nor the client can provide a finished objective account of a self as an existing being. The "thinking-about" a person that will truly reveal that person as an individual will not be distanced or disinterested—indeed, it *cannot* be—but will acknowledge its sources and allow itself to be drawn back through existence for validation. The individual who can keep abstract thought in existential perspective will be educated by it.

Summary

Traditional dualisms that feature "objective" and "subjective" domains are often objectivist through and through; the experienc*ed* is divided into "internal" and "external" content, and the experienc*ing* is ignored. The experienced is separated into types of content rather than distinguished from the experiencing, which is true subjectivity—the tissue of life of an existing person that yields that individual's unique style of being oriented in the world. When experiencing is properly grasped, it prohibits a detachment of thought from lived experiencing and gives us our world as one that is never totally transparent to nor encompassed by abstract thought.

Subjective knowledge is not an intellectualized knowledge limited to true propositions that purport to correspond to and articulate that which they are about. It is a knowledge marbled with the brute qualities of experiencing—the "what" is amplified by the "how." The self that is involved in a judgment informs that judgment with its involvement, yet no full view of the self is ever achieved by any set of judgments. Reflecting on the immediacies of experiencing gains only another "reflected"; the prereflective immediacy slips by and leaves reflection as a mode of knowing inherently detached from life-as-lived. As such, reflective objectivity is inadequate as an exclusive orientation for psychotherapy.

Abstract thought quickly becomes calculating thought (adding up all the objective information) because it cannot adequately deal with the complex disruptions in human existence that compel a person to seek therapeutic intervention. It attempts to bring about closure and control over that which it *does* contact so that it can build impressive systems that will disguise the fact of its inadequacy. Yet this loses facets of experiencing that are not abstractly conceptualizable. When general essences become the exclusive raw materials for theory building, only a limited type of therapeutic exchange is possible. The sacrifice of therapeutic effectiveness for the illusion that an objectively construed unity is synonymous with the universe is hardly justified.

To avoid a misrepresentation of human reality and to gain maximum fidelity for greater therapeutic effectiveness, the therapist must recognize the interplay of both subjective and objective dimensions. The professional clinician can then allow for a greater communicational exchange and a richer spectrum of therapeutic possibilities. If subjectivity is disallowed, human existence is transformed into a passionless artifact and the client is not regarded or treated as a complete human being.

The relevance of the above discussion for practicing therapists is more evident in actual cases. The following chapters describe a number of persons for whom self-blindness or self-disownership has become a serious hindrance in their everyday functioning. Their cases show clearly how the apprehension of subjectivity in therapy is not only important but often essential to therapeutic intervention. Indirect communication, and thus Kierkegaard's description of double reflection and metaphorical mirroring, plays a strong part.

3

Human Possibility and Metaphor

The How/What Dialectic

Paul was a timid adolescent. He was unsure what he wanted from therapy and even more unsure what he wanted from life. He shuffled uneasily as he came in the room and took an inconspicuous chair. His presenting symptom was lack of motivation in his school-work (he was a freshman at a small college).

The first task requested of him was to sit down and draw his family. Nervous about the activity, Paul eventually settled into it. He portrayed a large, frowning father, a brother almost as tall, and a thin, fragile-looking mother. He handed the paper to the therapist.

"You didn't include yourself," said the therapist. "You're part of the family, aren't you?"

Paul took back the drawing and sketched out a tiny figure next to his mother. "That's me," he said.

Interested, the therapist requested an additional drawing: a sketch of the house in which Paul and his family lived. Paul seemed more at ease with this one, although his skills were primitive. The boxy house and simple trees looked like something from a second-grade art class. The therapist looked it over. Suddenly Paul grabbed it from him with a cry of, "I forgot something!" He quickly added a window on the right side. "That's my room," he said, blushing over his mistake.

The patterns of self-belittlement remained constant throughout Paul's activities and descriptions. He portrayed a family life in which he stayed in the shadows in family discussions. When asked what sort of animal he might be if he woke up as one, he replied, "A fly." His girlfriend, he complained, seemed to derive great pleasure from ridiculing him in public, although he did not dare to request more respect from her. He had few friends, and those he had chosen often used him as a target for pranks.

It became clear to the therapist that Paul wanted someone to diagnose him, to tell him who he was and what to do. He did not wish to assert himself because he did not feel that his own decisions were to be trusted.

The therapist collected the evidence of Paul's poor self-regard for some time before he presented the full picture to Paul.

"Don't you see," said the therapist, "how you continually trip yourself up in all of your relationships and endeavors by running yourself down?"

Paul shook his head, clearly confused.

The therapist painstakingly outlined the patterns of self-deprecation: his choice of friends, his choice of girlfriend, his lack of family participation, how he "forgot" himself in his drawings. The list was long but consistent. Paul only shrugged.

"That's not what I'm doing," he said.

The therapist tried again, and failed, to get Paul to see that it was indeed what he was doing. Paul just did not buy the diagnosis.

Paul's case is a good example of how a person can fail to see his own behaviors simply by disowning them. Paul had falsified his experiencing by blocking out that which he did not wish to recognize. In Paul's case, to have agreed with the therapist's conclusions would have entailed taking on responsibility for himself, recognizing what he had done and what he should do now. He was not prepared for that—just one more pattern in the series. By not acknowledging what the therapist told him, he was able to nestle further into his self-detraction and, consequently, further into his self-deception about those activities that he failed to recognize as his own.

Ironically, that the therapist *told* him about himself gave Paul an additional opportunity to bury himself deeper into his myopia. Having heard the words, he was in a position to fling them back, disowning his experiencing verbally. This act strengthened his posture of self-blindness. The words, while referring to his manner of involvement with himself, failed to express the totality of the situation. The therapist failed to apprehend, then give back to Paul, the full structure of his experiencing. Instead he gave Paul an opportunity to further distance himself from himself. What Paul needed and failed to receive was a means by which to regain a lived awareness of himself—a sense of his own presence in what he was doing; he needed to regain his "memory."

Who Paul is in his subjective engagements cannot simply be told to him because the immediacy of his lived world sifts through the permeable web of words-as-names. He needs a mirror of sorts that will preserve *how* he is so that he can experience his self-neglect without the cognitive escape offered by conceptual mediation. In Paul's case, direct reference did little more than push him more solidly into his neurotic symptoms.

Paul's situation reveals the possibility for any of us to falsify our own personal mode of being. We live a certain way but have the capacity to disown some aspect that we may wish to avoid. This possibility gives us a glimpse into the human condition, one that shows how easily we can fall into a lie about ourselves *without really knowing* that we have done so. We can be self-deceived simply by existing. It is just another easy step to an annoying or even debilitating neurosis, like self-induced nausea, an inability to go into an open field, or a compulsion to drive home three times every day to assure ourselves that the coffeepot is unplugged. This sort of self-blindness is embedded in the very nature of subjectivity. Consequently, a detailed investigation of subjectivity has important ramifications for therapy.

Subjectivity—how an individual participates in his or her world—is not a hidden substance within the individual. That is, it is not a state of affairs that could, in principle, be directly expressible, but it is rather an on-going manner of engagement with situations in which persons find themselves. The best that abstraction can do with this engagement process is to capture it as general possibility. Yet human existence is not exhaustively depicted nor necessarily clarified through generalization. One's own meaningful participation in the world cannot be rendered in total as a directly expressible product because it is partially constituted by immediacies that precede and are not susceptible to abstraction and descriptions: "It [immediate experiencing] might be totally non-conceptual and fundamentally changed when it is grasped conceptually" (Scott 1982, 2). That which precedes, contributes to, but then escapes objective consciousness should be granted some recognition on its own terms in any knowledge that purports to be about human existence.

Experiencing feeds into the experienced, and in the dialectical relation between them there is no definitive boundary. The phenomena of human reality are present as a blend of both, and our own relations to the phenomena should represent them in their fullness. *What* Paul was doing in belittling himself to the point of dysfunctional confusion had experiential constituents. It *felt* a certain way to him, even though he had effectively blocked himself from acknowledging *how* it felt. In a more experience-oriented, and less linguistic-oriented approach, another therapist might have been able to catch Paul off his guard long enough to push him into that experiencing and thus to expand his restricted awareness of himself. That which we *can* apprehend of our experiencing should be allowed to inform our depiction of the experienced.

In therapy, allowing individuals to be present as complete persons can involve the therapist and client in a uniquely creative exchange. A complex matrix develops between them in which subjective and objective dimensions of the personal being of both participants mingle, blurring linguistically drawn distinctions. The experiencing of the therapist, merging into the way the therapist thinks about what he or she experiences, provides a testing ground for clients to experiment with the "how" and "what" of *their* experiencing. Let us posit a case and work our way through this sort of exchange, drawing in concepts previously introduced.

A general description of the case introduces Diane, who complained of a number of vague physical ailments—headache, tension, daily nausesa—and that she felt disoriented about herself and about life in general. She was frightened, she said, but was unable to pinpoint a direct cause for her fear. She did not relate well to others, including her family, and complained that she had no sense of "who" she was. She found that she was unable to make important decisions that required either a major commitment or some self-assertive action on her part. She claimed that she felt no purpose.

Events in Diane's life underlined her presenting symptoms. She had failed to complete either of two college degrees that she had begun. She jumped in and out of relationships with men because she was, as she described herself, afraid to become "settled." The only type of work in which she seemed capable of being employed was of a transient nature; she could not bring herself to look for a full-time, stable job, although she often spoke of the need to do so. She was interested in religion but not certain that anything she heard was "true." She had retained most of her friendships for only short periods of time. In less than two years Diane had gone through four therapists, claiming to derive little benefit from any of them, although it appeared to her current therapist that she had "jumped ship" just before intervention might have been effective. She displayed a strong repugnance toward any type of finalized project. Although she talked of a desire for a stable family life, many of her dreams were filled with family dissensions and deep fears about having children. For example, she had a dream in which she had a baby and kept it in a room through which all of her relatives passed, picking up the baby and fondling it, while Diane herself rarely entered the room.

Diane talked most about her sour relationship with her over-protective mother, claiming that she disliked most of her mother's characteristics and values but finding it impossible to break away from her. The relationship was replete with tension, evident both in Diane's description of it and in her manner of describing it. It became clear to Diane's therapist that one of her primary areas of difficulty was that she was unable to make commitments or take important actions that she perceived her mother might reject, although she insisted that she had no respect for her mother's values. It appeared to the therapist that Diane had so strongly internalized her mother's value system, while at the same time being repulsed by it, that she inadvertently prevented herself from making decisions that would help her to develop interests and values of her own. Diane rejected this diagnosis, denying hotly that she cared anything about what her mother had to say. Yet continued patterns in her words and behavior betrayed that the opposite was true.

This case as described allows the reader to note *what* the therapist said about the client—the collected content of the client's experience from regular meetings over a six-month period. Nothing is shown in the actual diagnosis of the nature or degree of participation of either the therapist or the client. Yet the difficulty of exposing subjective involvement is precisely this: to write it all out—to describe it thoroughly for a reader—is to objectify it, to make it an object for the reader's comprehension. It would be like trying to introduce someone to the color black by showing that person the color white and describing black as "the opposite." A great deal of detailed description of a client's situation *is* possible—much more than is evident in the paragraphs above—but neither the client's nor the therapist's experiencing of that which is described can be exhaustively delineated in the description.

While it may be objected that *nothing* is ever fully describable, some things are more grossly indescribable than other, that is, we do not get *any* conceptual grasp on experiencing in its lived immediacy because, by its very nature, it appears to elude the fragmenting effect of words as reference. Neither therapists nor clients have complete access to their *own* experiencing, much less to each other's. Yet each does have more access than mere linguistic description allows.

In the matrix that develops between therapist and client, it is possible for one to perceive more of the other's mode of engagement than the other does. Thus, the therapist may perceive more of the client's experiencing—or perceive it more clearly—than the client does, as Paul's therapist perceived obvious patterns that Paul refused to acknowledge. In addition, the therapist can help the client see where the client had heretofore been blind. How is this possible, especially since the experiencing cannot be simply conveyed through description? The answer is found primarily in the nature of the relations between persons that are developed in the social milieu of a culture.

Ambiguity and the Merging of Persons

Because of the elusive process-nature of experiencing, there is no direct, exhaustive correspondence between events and our specifications of them in language. Some features of a situation are not linguistically predicable. Attempting to depict a situation objectively can, in fact, be a way of obscuring it. In Paul's case the stated diagnosis of his symptoms not only failed to elicit acknowledgement from him but allowed him to push the symptoms even further away. Our minds may grasp something of the experiential phenomena, but when struggling to enclose it in linguistic expression, we leave out the "how" of the mind's grasping. That which is left out may have a significantly negative effect. Modifications of perception of the same content occur under different conditions, or in different persons. The same design can be seen as a duck or a rabbit, depending on the perceiver's mode of experiencing it. Philosopher Alastair Hannay (1979), discussing Kierkegaard's distinctions between content and manner of engagement, tells us:

> The world of experience is the kind of world that can be the expression of the experiencing subject's situational and conceptual viewpoint. . . . The "what" is not straightforwardly a world of common things in the way assumed by our concept of the world as providing a common vista. It is not a world that can be specified independently of what is special to the modes of individual minds. (26)

The way something is wrapped up in concepts cannot prevent the personal *manner* of "thinking-about" from finding an expression *of sorts* in the end product.

The elusive qualities of experiencing prevent straightforward, subjectively uncluttered delineations; ambiguous possibilities are implied in the apprehension of that which is linguistically conveyed. This ambiguity is described by Merleau-Ponty (1962) as the result of our bodily materiality. Accordingly, consciousness is not a disengaged spectator but is brought to life within an embodied self. The individual conditions of existence prevent "reality accounts" from having ideal lucidity. We are inevitably immersed in the very situations that we perceive and upon which we reflect. Experiencing blocks total clarity. Conscious intentionality blends into and threads through our lived involvements. The attitude that objectivity is certainty is only an attempt to escape the inevitable ambiguity, but such escape is impossible as long as consciousness is embedded in an existing individual. Bodily existence serves both the presence and absence of consciousness by being both an object for it and—in one way or another—the ground for its possibility, which cannot be its object. The bodily groundedness of human perception is a limitation of perspective. By simply looking around the room, the reader can sense the truth of this: how objects blur on the borders of perception, how a person who looks like a friend from a distance turns out to be a stranger. This experience is a dramatic contrast to the ideal clarity claimed for "perspective-free" science. The contrast, in turn, highlights the importance of lived experience over theoretical purifications in the clinical situation.

Ambiguity pervades our perceptions of ourselves. Consciousness of myself is embedded in the lived immediacies of my own manner of being in my world. My self-awareness fans out to envelope more than what I can say of myself; I cannot grasp myself completely through objective reflection. To say that I am depressed conveys *something* to a listener, but fails to do more than simply name an experience that is not as enclosed in the name as it sounds. To put a name to my state of mind (or body) is like trying to contain water in a sieve; the water keeps flowing. I look to others to aid me in my communication, because my involvement with others has contributed to "how" and "what" I am. Other people will understand me more readily and more completely by calling on an awareness of their own experiencing of depression rather than by relying on linquistic naming conventions.

Bruce Wilshire (1982) developed a theory of this sort of intimate human contact. To understand ourselves, he claims, we must first do so in general terms. Our development takes place through a series of imitative involvements; what we can be is exemplified in types of persons and in a variety of communication conventions. We see what others do and we do it.

> I cannot grasp myself without grasping myself as expressive to and for others, and without grasping my expression in terms of their expressive response to it. . . . Actions of mine recognizable through others' recognition of them are actions which are generally recognizable (are of the sort others would do), hence some must be mimetic of others' actions. . . . I must mime what others do and say about things if I am to learn about things, and so I must mime others continually. (165–66)

If I am attending, for the first time, a music recital, I look around to see how others in the audience act. They sit quietly, their eyes to the stage. I mimic them, and I am accepted as part of the audience. If I snore, talk, laugh, clap at the wrong time, or tap my fingers distractingly, the others let me know, with glares or other gestures of disapproval, that I am no longer acting appropriately, I am no longer "one of them."

These general modes confirm and authorize us in our developing humanity. Each person is initially engulfed in universals as "possibility-for-me." Individuals experience themselves through others as the others display themselves in various ways. It is assumed (not as self-evident, but as a result of observation) that a self is essentially educable and open to the impressions of others. Individuals are influenced by the personal examples and thoughts of others, and they appropriate values expressed by others; individuals develop their relations to others and to themselves through those others. Communal aspects of life are thus cocreated and our identifications are accomplished through mimetic recognitions. Each person is for and by others such that there is no distinctly objective center to one's world. Meaning is shared and fluid.

An individual is precipitated as such out of this initial group conformation. Basic ideas of persons as selves are derived from their relations to others such that they have no distinct "self" locked into a distinct body. The self is ambiguous; there are no clear boundaries between one self and another because we are too closely involved with each other. It is difficult to detect these mimetic involvements with others because they are incorporated primarily into areas of our consciousness about which we are not explicitly aware, such that they become automatic, habitual parts of our self expression. People are what they are in part because of the others who are unconsciously imitated (although how much cannot be definitely determined), and there are no means by which individuals can separate their "otherness" from their own individuality. Yet all persons *are* individuals, not just because they are housed in distinct bodies, but because they have distinct perspectives: there are limitations on their abilities to imagine the spectrum of human possibilities for themselves. One's experiencing, then, is one's own experiencing. One's body and one's perspective endow the individual with concrete actuality.

The peculiar nature of our involvement with others makes the way in which we engage in the world evident to others even when it is hidden to us by our lived involvement with ourselves. For example, I may have a tendency to view events in my life pessimistically: I think the worst when I go to a doctor; I am always sure I flunked a test; I tense up at an unexpected phone call; I take a hurried exchange as a sign of a deteriorating friendship. My closeness to these attitudes may blind me to them, just as Paul was blind to his self-depreciation. Yet another person could detect the pattern without much trouble. The other cannot *live* my experiencing as I live it. How can anyone else see it more clearly than I can?

Other people can be present to my experiencing through their own insofar as mine is, to some degree, like theirs. And since they do *not* live my experiencing as I do, they may not be put off by it as I might be were I to see it clearly. Nor are they fully engulfed in it, or overly intellectual about it. That which I fail to notice about myself because of my immediate experiencing of it, or because I have abstracted myself away from it or repressed it, can still be evident to others because I still live it and because it shows, more or less, in my mannerisms. That I am like others allows them a sympathetic sensitivity to me. They live their experiencing in like manner, given the influence of a common social and cultural upbringing and a continuous exposure to common ways of thinking. The experiencing of one person can be utilized to penetrate the experiencing of another.

Persons as Metaphors

As human beings who share a common social and cultural milieu, we are all like each other to some degree. Diane's therapist understood her because they shared language and socially recognizable behaviors and attitudes. As one person's experiencing allows that individual to respond to another's, the need for a direct (linguistically mediated) communication for that response diminishes. As the individual develops a better sense of the other person through repeated instances, he or she can begin to formulate a way to mirror back to the other that which has been perceived by the observer. Yet to do so the individual must provoke in the other an awareness of the other's own engagement that is not fragmented through the mode of abstract verbal reference. The other must be startled by the full, lived image of himself or herself in another person: "That's like me!" Such a response is derived from within the recipient's immediate engagements. The recipients do not think through *how* what they see is like themselves; they simply react to it because it is.

A woman whose son had been kept in a boy's home for several years for destructive behavior was in group therapy with other parents under similar circumstances. Time and again she complained that it was unfair, that she wanted her son to come home *now*. One member of the group pointed out to her that she was much like her son: a spoiled little kid, unable to take on the responsibilities of adulthood. She was stunned. She recognized herself in her son through the similarities in their immature, demanding responses to their situations. She took note of herself in spite of herself, through the powerful confrontation of lived recognition.

How we are metaphors for one another can be understood more

clearly through the analogy with theatre. Actors and their audience are in each other's presence as bodily selves. They *feel* one another. Actors disclose human types as they perform: they *enact* human possibility for an observer. What an actor discloses invites repeated instantiation, additional enactments by others: "He [the actor] stands in for each of us. He models a response to a difficult situation which, in one form or another, might befall any of us" (Wilshire 1982, 22). The response of the audience authorizes actors in their portrayals. If they recognize themselves, the actors are on target. In turn, an actor authorizes the audience to behave in a given way to a situation by doing so himself in his role. Hamlet portrays so well the ambivalence involved in thoughts of murder and revenge that audiences have resonated to his character in all ages and in many cultures. The audience identifies with him, and he with them. Wilshire describes this exchange:

> Theatre is the paradigmatic mimetic art and it deals with paradigmatically mimetic features of human life. The actor stands in for the character. But the character is a type of humanity with whom the audience member can identify, either directly as a stand-in for his own person, or indirectly as a stand-in for others whom the audience member recognizes, and with whom he can be empathetically involved. (1982, 22)

The success of the actor's being like some type of person depends to a large degree on the recipient. If the actor has captured the meaning of being human in particular situations, the recipient, as a human being, should respond. The audience is not guarded—after all, it is "only a play"—and should thus freely respond to that which exposes them to themselves. What the actor does can supply parts that are missing from a person's sense of his of her own experiencing. An actor deliberately lays down a detailed mode of human participation and the audience member reacts or responds undeliberately: the recipient senses himself or herself through something that bears life-similarities. That which has been hidden to the individual—absent in his or her self-awareness—is called forcefully into presence.

It is not that we place the actor in our world and live through him or her. Rather, we are returned to our own world as it is mediated through the actor's "world." The actor and the stage world are physiognomic metaphors: we *see* and *feel* them in their likeness to us. These metaphors put us "in touch with things that are too far or too close for us to see in our ordinary offstage life" (Wilshire 1982, 94). We sense ourselves fleshed out and we resonate to our own life as it is brought into focus through enactment. We are enabled to grow more open to ourselves through a revealing restructuring of our own engagements in a world.

Such is the role of the therapist. Therapists can serve as mirrors to the client when they use their own subjectivity to detect the experiencing of the client. They can then in some way enact that which they perceive in the client. If a client comes in and sits down rigidly in a chair, the therapist can sit rigidly, letting the client see himself or herself in the mirroring posture of the therapist.

Imitation is only one form of metaphor available to the therapist. Philip Barker (1985) gives a more exhaustive list:

> Elaborate stories designed to deal comprehensively with particular clinical situations; anecdotes and shorter stories designed to achieve limited therapeutic goals; analogies, similies and brief metaphorical statements or phrases used to emphasize specific points; relationship metaphors . . .; rituals and tasks with metaphorical meanings; and artistic metaphors—artistic productions representing things of clinical significance. . . . In addition, objects themselves may be used metaphorically. . . . (62–63)

A more detailed use of metaphor in therapy follows in chapter 5. First, it is important to explore the general dynamics of metaphor, which will lead into Kierkegaard's understanding of indirect communication.

Metaphor

Metaphoric unity is multivalent and rich with meaning; it admits of many senses not open to unambiguous logic. The structure of human experiencing can only be properly represented in a form congruent with the complex manner in which it is lived. The ambiguity of metaphor, then, has possibilities for preserving an experiencing that is also marbled with ambiguity. Metaphor draws ideas through patterns but then leaves them unfinished; the ideas must be finished in the recipients' own lived sense of themselves in their worlds. There is no limit to what a metaphor might call to our attention, and its isomorphic relation to human existence has the power to allow individuals to notice a number of new aspects of that which is revealed to them. That which awakens them to themselves through fully structured similarity provides new perspectives: "In having recourse to metaphor, then, a person provides either himself or others with a way of conceiving or imagining something from a different, if not a new, perspective: a perspective not ordinarily taken" (Murray 1975, 296).

With metaphor, "seeing as" is not "seeing that." It is not *about* structures seen in perspective, but *allows* indefinitely many levels of meaning. That which one apprehends through metaphor is worked out through experiential gestalts. A vaguely structured, amorphous experience might be made forcefully intelligible with a similar but more structured depiction, for example, to say that my relief is like a child climbing from my shoulders gives the experience a concrete clarity. Our imagination is supplemented: we can be lead or tickled or shocked into "seeing."

Kierkegaard exploits the notion in his creation of his many pseudonyms that persons can serve as such mirrors for other persons. Many of his books are either authored or edited (or both) by fictional personas. The names Johannes Climacus, Hilarius Bookbinder, and Johannes Anti-Climacus are not just labels for different books. They are meant to be perceived by readers as persons in their own right. Like an actor, Kierkegaard creates characters whose styles of life can be poetically observed and repeated, or "reduplicated." He taps basic human experiencing to offer fleshed out perspectives through which he believed personal values are typically developed. He creates possibilities for others to enact in their own lives. He wrote a treatise in the way that he imagined it might be written by a particular person engaged in the world in a particular way. The structure of human experiencing is captured with a fictional but similar-to-true-life structure and displayed in such a manner that readers can learn about themselves without being told anything directly. The characters have a suggestive illocutionary force that presses readers back into themselves; they are promptors, getting the reader to "read solo the original text of the individual human existence-relationship, the old text, the well-known, . . . to read it through yet once more, if possible in a more heartfelt way" (Kierkegaard [1846] 1968, 554). The conditions of becoming a person are condensed into perceivable patterns, intensifying the impact on individuals who acknowledge the relation to themselves. The content is grasped in virtue of its experienceability.

Readers are stretched through these incarnated thought-experiments; their lives are disturbed out of habitual dullmindedness. They see a likeness of themselves through the similar modes of another person—albeit a fictional one—and they cannot easily escape what they see. Kierkegaard deliberately designed his characters to be like general types of people, but types with flexibility for variation. He wanted readers to come to his works as they would go to a mirror—to see what was there, whether or not they wanted to. That people are like each other and can thus be revelations for each other allows his literature to work in the way he had hoped. More will be said about the pseudonyms when indirect communication is discussed in detail in the following chapter.

The use of metaphor in therapy is not new or innovative. A number of therapists have utilized the flexible and ambiguous structure of metaphor to get messages across to clients, although the actual literature is sparse (Barker 1985). Milton Erickson was the originator of extensive use of indirect techniques for clinical purposes. He firmly believed that he was able to treat clients successfully without requiring psychological explanation, argument, or client insight.

Believing that therapy should be "interesting and appealing," Erickson developed a variety of devices that would serve to model the worlds of his clients and stimulate them to create solutions to their problems. He used metaphors extensively to facilitate a search and retrieval process of personal learnings and abilities on the part of the client. Of his approach, Erickson said:

> When you understand how a man really defends his intellectual ideas and how emotional he gets about it, you should realize that the first thing in psychotherapy is not to try to compel him to change his ideation; rather you go along with it and change it in a gradual fashion and create situations wherein he, himself, willingly changes his thinking. (Erickson 1980, 335)

Erickson wanted to meet his clients through their own models of their world and to develop a deep rapport. He often used "teaching tales" to analogue a person's situation and then to suggest possible solutions. For example, for clients who might indulge in chronic self-pity, Erickson had the following anecdote:

> I spent one summer grubbing up brush on ten acres of land. My father plowed it that fall and replanted it, replowed it in the spring and planted it into oats. . . . Late that summer, my father examined the oat stalks and said, "It will be at least one hundred bushels per acre. And they will be ready to harvest next Monday."
> And we were walking along happily thinking about a thousand bushels of oats and what it meant to us financially. It started to sprinkle. It rained all night Thursday, all day Friday . . . Saturday . . . and Sunday. When we were finally able to wade through the water to the back field . . . there weren't any upright oats.
> My father said, "I hope enough of the oats were ripe enough so that they will sprout. In that way we will have some green feed for the cattle this fall—and next year is another year." (Rosen 1982, 235–36)

Erickson believed that therapeutic change resulted from helping clients reorganize and reassociate their experiences so that their own resources became available in new ways. Therapeutic suggestions were interspersed in stories whose content was seemingly removed from the clients' concerns. When clients were able to view themselves via metaphor (in the context of "someone else's" situation), they felt no need to guard themselves. They were open to the messages.

Erickson regarded his technique as a utilization of unconscious learning (viewing the unconscious as the accumulation of preconscious experiences in the unfocalized, elusive margins of consciousness, much as Kierkegaard did). Typically his indirect approach was brought into play after he had induced a naturalistic trance state in which the clients might become more attuned to holistic experiencing. He believed that clients already had the resources they needed; they just failed to recognize them, limited by conscious beliefs and habitual behaviors. "They know, and they don't know that they know" (Wilk 1985, 212).

A number of Erickson's colleagues and disciples have attempted to offer explanations and explicit frameworks for his approach. Haley (1973) views the use of metaphor as a way to eliminate the possibility of reductionistic interpretations of a client's situation. The therapeutic intervention opens up into a multiplicity of meanings, allowing the client more flexibility for interpreting his or her problem. Wallas (1985) calls the teaching tales "stories for the third ear," following Nietzsche's reference to the "third ear" as a means by which we hear the metaphorical language of our intuition. Zeig (1980) explains the basic properties and functions of anecdotes, calling attention to the manner in which these stories foster hypnotic responsiveness through nonthreatening "packaging." Lankton and Lankton (1983), former students of Erickson, provide an analysis of Erickson's *multiple embedded metaphors*. Gordon (1978) deals with the development of metaphor in various specific contexts of therapy, moving from one case to another to illustrate the flexibility and general effectiveness of indirect communication.

Most of the work done on metaphor has been from those clinicians associated with Erickson. However, there are other fine examples. Bandler and Grinder (1979), in their presentation of Neurolinguistic Programming, a language-based therapy, use metaphors to illustrate and facilitate modes of communication among persons that include visual, auditory, and kinesthetic responsiveness.

Probably the most famous use of metaphor comes from Gestalt Therapy (Perls 1969). Role-playing, dream analysis, and the "empty chair" device are among the means through which clients are encouraged to "get in touch" with their feelings, with their here-and-now immediacies. Gestalt Therapy explores the phenomenon of levels of awareness. Translated literally, *gestalt* means the configuration of the whole. Each aspect of a person's functioning has meaning only in context of the whole of his of her experiencing. Believing that most of us are fragmented, Perls's goal is reintegration, to encourage clients to take on parts of themselves toward which they have become alienated. The healthy person experiences life as a meaningful whole, with smooth transitions between figure (immediate focal awareness) and background (marginal subjectivities).

Many of the theories that shoot forth into indirect techniques have a common denominator in Kierkegaard. All of them echo his concern for psychologically crippled self-blindness and the need for holistic rather than fragmenting treatment. His elaborate philosophical framework gives explanatory power to the clinical procedures, and his rich descriptions complement, and are complemented by, the cases offered in the therapeutic literature. He touches on the metaphorical dynamic in a profound and revealing way. Before laying out Kierkegaard's thought, however, one more important aspect of the general dynamic of metaphorical communication must be covered.

The Importance of Unstructured Awareness

That which one person communicates metaphorically to another is most fully present to a recipient whose awareness is open and free of conceptual hindrances. Thus, therapists who want to exploit the similarities among persons to help a client gain self-awareness must first be flexible in their own self-awareness. This is neither an automatic nor an easily attained achievement, however; it requires concentration, self-examination, and a great deal of discipline. Habitual thought patterns and implicit biases are difficult to shake off, and they can bar much from a therapist's perception. In the case of Paul, the therapist thought the best approach was simply to spell it out for Paul. It failed to work. Should the therapist persist in this procedure, continued failure is likely, as well as further aggravation of Paul's difficulties.

In addition, therapists caught up in prejudices may selectively attend to phenomena that concur with those prejudices. They may not see what *is* there, or they may see what is *not* there. For example, a behaviorist may view behavior as evidence of a person's state of mind (if the concept of a mind is appreciated at all), and thus fail to realize that we can purposely deceive someone about our state of mind via behavior, as well as have thoughts and feelings that are not expressed behaviorally at all. Modes of interpretation are persistent, however; they organize our perceptions along given boundary lines, and therapists need to understand just how their own beliefs play into the therapeutic situation. Otherwise, they will fail to see anything but what their beliefs allow them to see, and consequently might miss much of what is actually happening within the matrix developed between themselves and their clients.

There *is* an awareness between organized fields of mental concepts—the excess dough around the cookie cutter—an awareness that can broaden the therapist's overall comprehension. To gain access to it, structured mental habits must be relaxed. This may be frightening initially since it allows an enveloping mental state that seems aimless and ungrounded, perhaps even out of control: "As we step back from the event and allow it in its happening, its presenting, communicating occurrence, we undergo a subtle experience of fundamentally not being in control. We feel passage, horizon without resolution, inconstancy, an excess of the particularities . . . (Scott 1982, 138).

This amorphous feeling is uncomfortable for those who desire control. Yet to cling to a structuring consciousness for the purpose of control is to forfeit real control for only the illusion of it. A structuring consciousness allows us to believe we have a mental grasp of all states of affairs when in fact we have simply imposed an organization schema onto them that includes some and excludes others. If anything escapes such structures, the structuring consciousness forfeits control over it.

By letting go of our interests, we can flood ourselves with the immediacy of whatever comes forth; we can achieve awareness without conceptual interference. This is akin to responding openly to theatrical enactment, where expectations are bracketed as the audience waits to see what takes place. Developing such an awareness allows us to draw away from knowing the world and ourselves through generalities; we can acknowledge our own concrete situations. The indeterminateness and ambiguity of experiencing in its unthematized presence become evident to our awareness as the distinctions brought about by conceptual qualifiers and quantifiers are blurred; our own experiencing is allowed to be as it is prior to the domination of abstract reflection. We can be present to things that are absent to formal reflective modes of thinking. If we can develop a willingness to cancel our anticipations and expectations that are generated by our primary organizational structures, we can cultivate an awareness of experiencing that will penetrate those structures when they are in use.

What must be accomplished, then, for persons interested in utilizing indirect communication, is an alertness to their own sympathies and antipathies—to the spurs of their reactions and responses. What do they dismiss or cancel out automatically? What do they add? In other words, therapists who desire to develop an open alertness must attend to and gain knowledge of their own subjective involvement in their biased objective assessments and formulations.

Kierkegaard provides a bridge between a person's subjective and objective activities with his notion of double reflection. The double reflection is the reflection of inwardness, relating a person's thought to his or her existence. As stated in chapter 1 (and it bears repeating), it is the medium through which the metaphorical dynamic between persons works, as well as the channel for the awareness that is essential for the subject/object dialectic. However, since double reflection is so critically tied into Kierkegaard's description and use of indirect communication, a full analysis of both follows in the next chapter. Up to this point we have been primarily concerned with the possibility of expressing ourselves and reading the expressions of another without recourse to direct communication in words. This possibility has been shown to be achievable through the intuitive apprehension of others as being like us. The more open our awareness is, the more present we will be to what another can show us; and the more present we are to the other, the more we can see possibilities for ourselves. This is the basis for indirect communication. We need to be alert not only to the experiencing of the other, but also to our own.

Such a mode of intuitive attunement is useful to the therapist, as evidenced by Milton Erickson and his followers. The therapist can utilize objective disclosure when it is practical, but can also step away from it for a deeper awareness of the therapeutic situation. If the professional can transcend habitual engagements, he or she can gain a greater comprehension of the client's lived presence. If clients are closed off to their own experiencing, the therapist can find indirect ways to get the clients to see their own experiencing, which has been heretofore deserted. The client can be *startled* into self-awareness. Diane's case illustrates how some of these ideas apply.

Therapeutic Assessment of Subjectivity

Early in therapy, Diane was asked to draw a picture of her family. It was a simple request but one toward which she felt evident discomfort. She reluctantly agreed and set about the task. As she drew, she became quite nervous: she began to giggle, to erase erratically, and to smoke at a faster rate. Her face grew noticeably tense. The therapist noted all of these behaviors and, when she had finished, asked her to respond to what he had observed. She could not deny the evidence of the cigarette butts, but toward the rest of the information she reacted with only a blank expression. She seemed unable to recall her actual participation.

Since the therapist did not live her experiencing, he could not be absolutely certain about what he sensed. Yet he was present to something in her mode of activity that seemed to be clearer to him than it was to her. Why would he not simply take her overt denial of his observations and conclusions as an indication of the true state of affairs? He did not do so because his own experiencing of the situation prompted a different response on his part: he was initially surprised that she had denied what was so clearly evident in a physical way (tension, cigarette butts), but he was able to recover from this surprise to piece together a rationale for her blocked acknowledgement. What he saw in her was like what he had seen before, either in himself or in other clients. He understood her through something similar that gave him the basis for his rationale.

He could not adequately put what he knew into words, but he could allow it to feed into his mode of perceiving and interpreting. He believed his own perceptions to be accurate. However, rather than put a label on them right away, he stayed open to what she might show him in further sessions. He could not be certain that he was right, but he was reasonably confident in his professional training to make at least a tentative connection between what Diane appeared to be doing and what others do when they do not want to make their own engagements explicit to themselves. Thus, he exploited the similarities among persons to make sense of the behavior of his client. He did not, however, cut her off further from herself, nor did he cut himself off from her as a person by fitting her into a conceptually organized schema. He allowed *her* world to unfold. That is, *how* she engaged herself in the situation was in part evident to the therapist through his own experiencing. He could describe her engagement to some degree but he did not get caught up in objective categories such that he shriveled the awareness of her that allowed him a presence to her in the first place. And as much as he might try to describe her engagements to himself, he refrained from describing it to her because she had already closed off awareness of herself at a conceptual, referential level. Further reflection of an objective nature would not restore it.

The therapist needs to find another way to communicate to Diane her own distanced experiencing. He must find a "mirror." In this case, he cannot enact self-deception and self-abrogation to her. Yet he *can* utilize the human experiential connection that they share to find a way to get her to see herself as he sees her. A communication that exploits metaphor can both utilize and go beyond theatrical enactment. Such techniques are explored in the following chapters.

4
Kierkegaard's Indirect Communication

The Double Reflection

The communication of subjectivity requires that the communicator have the ability to note his or her own experiencing. This involves an awareness that is not drawn through verbal mediation. According to Kierkegaard, an individual reflects outwardly, toward and about the world, as well as inwardly, involving the self. In the *Postscript* ([1846] 1968), Kierkegaard says:

> But existence itself. . . keeps the two moments of thought and being apart, so that reflection presents him [the existing person] with two alternatives. For an objective reflection, the truth becomes an object . . . and thought must be pointed away from the subject. For a subjective reflection, the truth becomes a matter of appropriation of inwardness, of subjectivity, and thought must probe more and more deeply into the subject [the person]. (171)

Outward reflection constitutes objective thought, turning everything thought about into a directly expressible result of the thinking process; human experience is translated into ideas and concepts. The inward reflection—not really a "reflection" in the sense of "thinking about," but more like an intuitive awareness—links the ideas to the existence from which they were taken, probing "more and more deeply into the subject."

Any thinking process begins uniquely as that of an individual and can be so acknowledged with a more self-involved awareness by the thinking person. "An actual emphasis on existence must be expressed in essential form. . . namely, the absence of a system [of abstractions]" ([1846] 1968, 111). Kierkegaard describes this distinction:

> When the thought has found its suitable expression in the word, which is realized by means of a first reflection, there follows a second reflection, concerned with the relation between the communication and the author of it, and reflecting on the author's own existential relationship to the idea. ([1846] 1968, 71)

Individuals think about their world and also realize their own manner of engagement with it: "The subjective thinker," says Kierkegaard, "is as an existing individual essentially interested in his own thinking, existing as he does in his own thought" ([1846] 1968, 67). To understand oneself *as* a subject, one's own experiencing must be brought to one's lived awareness.

There is no direct linguistic expression for the second reflection by which to connect with other people for a general consensus about the nature of that experiencing; to try to use simple verbal reference for one's own actuality separates one from oneself through a type of mediating reflection, a separation that can be only conceptual, and thus potentially self-deceptive. "Even in such moments of abstraction, the abstract thinker pays his debt to existence by existing in spite of all abstraction" (Kierkegaard [1846] 1968, 170). The quality of subjectivity defies direct description and expression because it is a mode of being that is never completely objectifiable. The finalities of direct expression fail to convey it, not because it is a "concealed inner substance," but because it is fluid, open-ended, and continuous. "The immediate never is as such, but is transcended as soon as it is" (Kierkegaard [1846] 1968, 102).

Inwardness cannot be translated into results because it is essentially process. "An existing individual is constantly in the process of becoming; the actual existing subjective thinker constantly reproduces the existential situation in his thoughts and translates all his thinking into terms of process" (Kierkegaard [1846] 1968, 79). Existence is the process of making possibilities real or actual for oneself, and an individual's relation to those possibilities is that person's manner of choosing to draw or not to draw them into his or her life. Thus, when persons simply reflect *about* something, their thinking is directed objectively; they can express this thinking in direct form. When they live what they experience they actualize it, giving it more embodiment than words-as-names can capture.

Direct description and expression is the use of verbal signs to refer to something. It is, in principle, public. That which is signified by some word or phrase is immanent in the sign (or reference) and is communicated via the sign:

> A man with knowledge of certain realities forms concepts that are mental symbols of those realities, and expresses what he thinks by means of words, which are spoken or written signs of his concepts. When a hearer or reader apprehends the verbal symbols, translates them into the concepts they stand for, and these in turn into the realities signified, the process is complete. (Mackey 1971, 246–47)

This is the direct route for communication, mediated through concepts.

However, when individuals reflect on their own relation to that which is thought about—how they are present in their thinking—another manner of reflection is required, one that focuses on the individual's mode of relating, on inwardness: "Objectively, the interest is focused merely on the thought-content, subjectively on the inwardness" (Kierkegaard [1846] 1968, 181). C. Stephen Evans (1978) clarifies this point: "The objective thinker seeks to understand a concrete reality by subsuming it under objective concepts; the subjective thinker seeks to understand an abstract concept in relationship to his own concrete existence as a particular human being" (79). The thinker as an existing individual is constantly in the process of becoming, and the personal relationship to his or her thinking must also be in process:

> Not for a single moment is it forgotten that the subject is an existing individual, and that existence is a process of becoming, and that therefore the notion of the truth as identity of thought and being is a chimera of abstraction... all essential knowledge is essentially related to existence. (Kierkegaard [1846] 1968, 176–77)

Thinking in the mode of the first reflection must always fail to capture its own processes because *it* is always in process. "Reflection cannot be stopped by itself, because in attempting to stop itself, it must use itself" (Kierkegaard [1846] 1968, 102). Every reflecting involves a reflecting that is not wholly grasped in the discrete acts of reflecting, like a river into which one cannot step twice.

The second reflection, then, provides a means of accessing directly lived experiencing, which is generally in the shadows of ordinary conceptual reflection. As Kierkegaard puts it: "The reflection of inwardness gives to the subjective thinker a double reflection. In thinking, he thinks the universal; but as existing in his thought and as assimilating it in his inwardness, he becomes more and more subjectively isolated" ([1846] 1968, 68). The reflection of inwardness is the awareness of thinkers that has doubled back on them in their relation to their thought; it holds them apart as individuals so that they do not coagulate with each other into a diluted general point of view by thinking only the universal. While thought-content itself is delivered into the general realm via a shared language, it cannot be entirely stripped of the individuality of the thinker.

The double reflection prevents consciousness from abstracting itself away from the immediacy of concrete human experiencing. It amounts to reflecting immediately on what is experienced in order to confront the *how* of the experiencing *as* it eludes objective reflection. We are enabled to apprehend our thought-products as they are situated in the here-and-now of our particular situations. For example, some aspects of Wilhelm Reich's personality theory can be convincingly construed as a savior fantasy derived from his mother's suicide (Atwood and Stolorow 1977). Alertness to the immediate blends into conceptual interpretation such that lived immediacies permeate all mediations of human existence. Awareness of oneself, of one's world, and of others is expanded, guiding and generating new dimensions of thought and of lived experience. While concepts retain their public accessibility in direct expression, their existence also admits to the fact of their abstraction by the individual who thinks them.

Heidegger (1962) postulates a condition in this regard that is purportedly part of all human attunements and moods: *befindlichkeit*, which means that one is always present to oneself, however inarticulately and obscurely. The self cannot escape itself, but must be attuned to its world in one way or another *as* a self so attuned. Because we feel as well as think about our world, we can be attuned to aspects of human reality that cannot be expressed in terms of ordinary objective cognition alone. Kierkegaard's double reflection heightens our awareness of our presence to ourselves and as such involves us interestedly in our thinking.

The second reflection, then, is an important bridge to self-development. The more self-aware we are, the more we can grow and change. For example, a tennis player who serves the ball awkwardly and who does not want to accept that about himself may think in the first level of reflection (which can distance himself from his experiencing) that he possesses a graceful serve. His reflection—a product of what he wants to believe about himself rather than a product of what he is actually doing—deceives him and prevents him from taking note of his actual style of engagement. A double reflection will confront his desire to believe something about himself that may not be true and will thus alert him to the possibility that he is deceiving himself; he may then pay closer attention to how he is actually serving the ball and may improve his serve. This has obvious implications for therapy.

In Diane's case, she believes something about herself that includes a failure to see her full lived involvement in her situation. The therapist wants to bring this to her attention to help her to work through it. However, if the therapist too is blinded by beliefs that truncate his perspective and has never worked them through, he may not understand Diane's situation well enough for effective intervention. Or he may not see the possibilities for reengaging her with herself.

Hannay (1979) believes that double reflection can be understood in two possible ways. The first interpretation shows inwardness to be a response by an individual who calls on all of his or her resources:

> It seems correct to say that the less a problem can be solved for you, and the more you are left to your own resources in solving it, the greater will be the extent of the relevance of your own particular circumstances and situation to a specification of the problem itself, as well as of its solution. (149)

Hannay's second possible meaning of the inward reflection is linked to the notion of worldviews, or principles according to which a perspective has been organized: "A life-view, for Kierkegaard, imparts a certain order on existence" (149). This order is *imposed* on existence, unjustified by anything but itself, and involves the individual in a "leap of faith": "A life-view is a kind of conjectural stab at a personally satisfactory organization of experience, though lacking the benefit of either objective proof or refutation" (150). One person's life-view is incommensurable with another's: "However internally consistent two life-views may be, they are mutually exclusive" (151). A life-view is not comprised of states of affairs that are exhausted by conceptual definition: "They are, as it were, something about, some subjective quality of, states of affairs and not either themselves states of affairs or having any basis in such" (152). Either interpretation, Hannay asserts, still leaves the problem of communication and the need for some means of expression other than verbal correspondence.

C. Stephen Evans (1983) also analyzes the second reflection. He questions whether the thought of the subjective thinker is essentially thought or essentially action. If it is strictly comprised of action, he contends, there would be no reflection; but then action would be blind, arbitrary, and chaotic. This is hardly what Kierkegaard is describing.

On the other hand, if the second reflection is essentially thought, the initial separation involved in making the connection between existence and reflection is problematic, making the second reflection akin to the first. Evans resolves this dilemma by showing that Kierkegaard draws one distinction between thought and action and another between thought that is concerned with action and thought that is not:

> Thought and action are both linked and separated by existence. Thought, no matter how closely connected with action, is never equivalent to action. . . .
>
> However, action is by no means devoid of thought . . . genuine action is the realization of what has been thought. This separation and linkage makes it possible for the individual to reflect on what he should do and thereby understand his action prior to acting. (99)

That is, it may be possible to understand what a schizophrenic psychosis is without having it, even though it is primarily a way of existing. When a client describes hearing voices telling him to kill himself, the therapist can grasp what that means without having to hear the voices too. This is possible because thought can be either abstract or concrete; concrete thought involves the thinker and a definite experiential context for understanding what is thought. Thus subjective thought—the second reflection—is not action but a relation to action, which distinguishes it from pure abstract thinking. It is linked to action by decision and commitment. As Kierkegaard puts it: "To think about existential problems in such a way as to leave out the passion is not to think about them at all; it is to forget the point, which is that the thinker is himself an existing individual" ([1846] 1968, 304).

The sharp distinctions that are conceptually apparent between thinking and acting do not appear in the experiencing of the thought-act complex: "To the person who has acted, her thought appears to her as the first phase of her action; her action is the realization of this thought . . . she sees her reflection and her action as the beginning and fulfillment of a single process" (Evans 1983, 304). The second reflection, then, is not a reduplication in existence of what is thought about, but the relating to the thought-about for the purpose of either reduplicating it in action or not. It is a means of drawing the "how" intimately into the "what," a *feel* for it rather than a "thinking about" it.

The Communication of Subjectivity

KIERKEGAARD'S INDIRECT COMMUNICATION

Double reflection is related to communication in that the first reflection allows the direct linguistic expression characteristic of objectivity and the second provides for the apprehension and indirect lived expression of subjectivity. Kierkegaard follows through on this relation in a succinct paragraph in the *Postscript*:

A double reflection is implicit in the very idea of communication. Communication assumes that the subject exists in the isolation of his inwardness. . . and desires at one and the same time to have his thinking in the inwardness of his subjective experience and yet also to put himself in communication with others. This contradiction cannot possibly find expression in direct form . . . because such form presupposes results and finality. Direct communication presupposes certainty [finished results]; but certainty is impossible for anyone in the process of becoming. The reflection of inwardness gives to the thinker a double reflection. . . .

The difference between subjective and objective thinking must express itself also in the form of communication suitable to each. . . . The subjective thinker will . . . have his attention called to the requirement that this form should embody artistically as much of reflection as he himself has when existing in his thought. ([1846] 1968, 68n)

Inwardness is of concern to individuals when they note it as much as possible in their thought. Because it is an essential influence in their thinking, they want to communicate it in the direct expression of the thought. However, a direct expression of their mode of relating to their thought is impossible because the continuous nature of that relating cannot use the medium of the finished products or words as reference.

With indirect communication, there is no automatic transition from a word to what it signifies, as there is from "tree" to a ready object in our world. There are no qualifiers to indicate static meaning. If there is a verbal language, it is not put to its conventional referential use: "Indirect communication occurs in the expansion of the interface between sign and referent and in the indefinite deferment of sense procured by the restless interplay of the signifiers" (Mackey 1981, 230). That which is absent in a cognitive communication of objective information is brought into presence with indirect communication in such a manner that the recipient is more than cognitively involved in the communication process. Dostoevsky *felt* the impact of what the other prisoner's disgruntled manner communicated to him. The inwardness of one individual can be apprehended by another and then communicated back to the individual without a loss of the immediacy of the inwardness: the experiencing of the one is grasped by another through the other's own experiencing and communicated back without leaving the medium of experiencing. Communicating inwardness indirectly generates a double reflection in the recipient so that personal, unique subjectivity becomes evident to individuals as they live it.

Kierkegaard regards communication as a multilayered process rather than as a conveyance of static information. He looks to the example of the Socratic maieutic as a pattern: "The reason why several of Plato's dialogues end without results is far more profound than I used to think. It is an expression of Socrates' maieutic art which makes the reader, or hearer himself active, and so does not end in a result but a sting" ([1846] 1942, 4:210). The communication does not convey asserted facts, but elicits a more visceral response through inwardly directed suggestion: "When in reflection upon the communication the receiver is reflected upon, then we have . . . the maieutic. The communicator disappears, as it were, makes himself serve only to help the other to become" ([1847] 1942, 1:292).

For Kierkegaard, a communication of results leaves the reader dependent on the author as the "authority" who asserted them. An indirect communication prohibits such a relation: "the true communicator recognizes the necessity to distance himself from the receiver, to help the receiver to grasp the truth on his own" (Evans 1983, 103). No one but the receivers are allowed authority over themselves. When they are struck inwardly by a communication, rather than only cognitively, they must look to themselves for interpretation and action: "An example of such indirect communication is, so to compose jest and earnest that the composition is a dialectical knot. . . . If anybody is to profit by this sort of communication, he must himself undo the knot for himself" (Kierkegaard [1850] 1941, 132–33). Thus the recipient is an active link, having a multifaceted potential for response. Witness to a truth is forced from within, as it was for the Christ-imitator who had to recognize his psychosis for himself.

The communicator cannot cause or prevent a given action. He or she merely provides an occasion for self-awareness on the part of the client (Evans 1983, 104). The recipient is responsible for decision and action because at some level an incongruence appears in the communication process and the participants are blocked from direct access to each other. The communicator *cannot* serve as authority. Kresten Nordentoft (1972) describes some of the many variations of this incongruence:

1) Incongruence between the object and the communication (the text); e.g., the intentionally negative irony which is attributed to Socrates.

2) Incongruence between the communicator and that which is communicated; e.g., becoming a teacher by denying that one is a teacher.

3) Incongruence between that which is communicated and the recipient; e.g., assuming something about the recipient which provokes him to a new self understanding. (346)

There may also be internal contradictions in any one of the constituents of the communication process. For example, an internal contradiction in the recipient might take the form of a self-deception, which would be manifested through denial reactions to a confronting communication.

Indirect communication should have the effect of a shock that pushes people away from their prereflectively engaged situation; in the distancing, they see the possible *qua* possible. Their perspective on themselves is expanded and broadened. They feel the visceral force of their own existence.

Two steps are involved in Kierkegaard's approach:

In the negative step, the recipient must first be cleansed, or dispelled of illusions that could block the perceptive insight necessary for the next step: "To communicate can thus mean to trick someone out of something" ([1847] 1942, 1:275). For example, the woman who wanted her son back had to face up to her own childish behavior before she was able to work out a satisfactory way of having the boy in her home.

In the positive step, the recipient is spurred toward self growth. "The real communication and instruction . . . is upbringing. By means of upbringing, one becomes what he is essentially regarded to be" ([1847] 1942, 1:279). That which an individual is to be is assumed to be already present in him or her; it is developed in this step of the process.

Essentially, therapists interested in utilizing indirect communication need to achieve one or more of the following strategies.

First, they need to repeat themes or patterns of a person's experiencing until he or she feels pressured to act on that which is shown to them about themselves. Continued renewal of a theme allows for deeper penetration of the theme. Diane might be told several different stories that bear on the theme of value-paralysis from various perspectives. Persons who are presented over and over again with the structure of their experiencing are enabled to see it more deeply or from changing perspectives. Repetition is almost essential to indirect communication: passing over something once makes it difficult to comprehend, especially when it is presented through the subtleties of an indirect communication. Repetition imposes a constancy for scrutiny on the flux of identity; without being a reexperience of the same theme or situation, it becomes a circle in which the self can work out its own consolidation: "Repetition is the self's recovery of itself" (Caputo 1982, 348). We are forced to renew an acquaintance with that part of ourselves that has been engulfed by daily life. Repeated self-examination allows a recovery of the lived quality of experiencing.

Second, therapists need to slow down the client's mode of engagement by creating a disturbance in it. Doing so will draw the client's attention away from ordinary reflection and toward his or her own manner of experiencing. For example, Paul's therapist might have requested that Paul walk more slowly into the room so that he would be more aware of which chair he had chosen. Paul might then have noted the reasons why he had selected that particular chair—reasons that can be easily obscured by blind habits of entering a room and sitting down.

Third, therapists need to abort the experiencing of the clients to keep it from its typical consummations. Diane's therapist might ask her to spend an important holiday by herself rather than go, guilt-compelled, to her mother's. He wants her to break a pattern. Another example of interrupting a person's lived engagements occurred when the woman who demanded that her son be allowed to come home was cut to the quick by another group member's single comment. This strategy should generate some frustration or dissatisfaction that might provoke the clients to take note of themselves in their typical modes of relating in their worlds. Basically, the communicator wants to expose presupposed conditions of personal identity so that the recipient can "see" without being told how or what to see; he or she can make self-discoveries and then take responsibility for them.

Indirect communication intends to bypass reflection and to liberate the recipients so that they can become self-reliant: "lovingly to help a person to the point at which he becomes himself free, independent, his own; to help him stand alone . . ." (Kierkegaard [1859] 1962, 255–56). The communicator wants simply to display possibilities to the recipients so that they will regard them in some relation to themselves. Recipients are not so much manipulated as disarmed of resistance and defense so that they can be offered what is their own.

As a form of communication, the indirect method draws on little objective data and makes no linguistic articulation of what is sensed in another person. The individuals involved retain their own distinct mode of experiencing as they relate themselves to the communication. The subjective thinker recognizes the doubleness characteristic of existence—the outward, objective universal and the inward, subjective particular. Subjective thinkers both live and think and allow their living to pervade their thinking. Existence thus requires both forms of communication to be preserved in its fullness.

As recipients of indirect communication reflect in a double reflection, they gain an awareness of their own presence in their thought and, when they exist reflectively in their thought, they can perceive something of how others are in *their* thought:

> The reception of inwardness does not consist in a direct reflection of the content communicated, for this is an echo. But the reproduction of inwardness in the recipient constitutes the resonance by reason of which the thing said remains absent. . . but inwardness is when the thing said belongs to the recipient as if it were his own. . . ." (Mackey 1971, 291)

The mode of another's engagement suggests itself through that to which the recipients can relate themselves and is thus known through their own experiencing; they "resonate" to the other person. Whatever is present to them is allowed to be as it is in its own form because they have become sensitive to a spectrum of expressive occurrences, which is broader than mere linguistic expression.

Indirect apprehension is never sure or secure. Inaccurate awareness or lack of perception on the part of either participant impedes the effectiveness and completion of a communication. Misunderstanding, frustration, and any number of other factors may intrude, and where there is no cognitive bridge, possibilities for inaccurate apprehension are multiplied. However, because the communication is typically embedded into some type of metaphorical device, less is lost than if it had been stated straightforwardly. The therapist is free to try again on the same theme through a different story or technique.

The communication may also fail because the recipient is free to think through or not think through the possibilities presented to him. However, an indirect communication is specifically designed so that the recipient will be compelled to take more than conceptual note of it. The more subtle the indirection, the greater the possibility that recipients will be responsive in spite of themselves, although subtlety can also bury the content. Indirection is an art, requiring a developed skill and a fine sense of existential balance.

Skill in attunement is another essential feature of this type of exchange. The communicator must be sensitive not only to the uniqueness of individual experiencing but also to that which is common to human inwardness. The commonalities allow one person to be a metaphor for another insofar as he or she is *like* the other. Indirection exploits this possibility.

Concentration both on oneself and on the other is also necessary to indirection. One's own self-awareness serves as the ground from which one can apprehend the lived immediacies of the other. If a therapist treating a man for marital problems fails to relate herself to her prereflective engagements through a double reflection, she creates a division between herself and aspects of her experiencing that may help her with her client. Then she is restricted to apprehending the man's situation through his verbal descriptions that inadequately capture the fully lived impact of his experiencing. She thus risks losing the immediacy of the other's lived engagement. A double reflection must also be provoked in the client for the communication to be completed. And the therapist must understand what this is in order to provoke it in her client. The experiencing of one individual is held away, to some extent, from anyone not doubly reflected to some degree in themselves.

KIERKEGAARD'S PSEUDONYMS

Kierkegaard offers many examples of indirect communication, most notably his pseudonymous fictional "authors." He also uses irony, humor, and parody in the form of parables and anecdotes. These techniques are meant to be pointers, directing readers to their own existence by revealing possibilities for decisive action:

> These modes of existence [the pseudonyms] Kierkegaard conceives as universal and objective in content. However, what he desired to do was not merely to describe these modes of existence in an objective way; what he wished to do was to communicate them in such a way that his readers would consider them subjectively, that is, with an understanding that these are possibilities which confront them as individuals for rejection or actualization. (Evans 1978, 80)

Kierkegaard uses the familiar in an unfamiliar way, creating a disruption in cognition through which subjectivity might leak. Human possibility is employed through stories or character portraits to force an issue—to create a private crisis in the life of a reader that can be resolved only by his or her own decision and action. "The reflection of inwardness which gives to the subjective thinker a double reflection . . . [must] embody artistically as much of reflection as he himself has when existing in his thought" (Kierkegaard [1846] 1968, 68n). By frustrating readers' normal expectations, he shows them that what they thought they understood was merely something with which they were familiar. The readers are challenged to reflect (in a double reflection) on the limitations of personal, habitual ways of understanding. They can then be alerted to avenues of self-understanding not normally available in their habitual modes: "Kierkegaard frustrates the reader's desire for 'results,' for closure that would put a false finish to a never-ending activity of pursuing meaning through understanding" (Armstrong 1981, 47). For example, when he offers a story without an interpretation or tells the parable about the drunken man who waved a passing cart over his own legs because he failed to recognize them as his own, Kierkegaard incites the readers to ponder the "message" for themselves and to make their own choices about it. He uses repetition of themes, metaphors in which the flow of experiencing is arrested for reflection, and surprising or humorous anecdotes to rupture routine ways of understanding or moving through life.

Readers are awakened to their freedom, called to heightened applications of their subjective powers for self-discovery. The truth is sought not in what is said but in *how* the person responds to it.

Kierkegaard wants to impose between himself and his reader an anonymous object that is so articulated that it has potential for an unlimited array of possibilities for the reader. He intends to "induct the reader into the implications of a world where 'truth' varies according to the activity of its producer" (Armstrong 1981, 40). Interpretation is dependent on the hermeneutical position of the person apprehending it. The writings comprise a mirror that is held up to the reader so that truth comes forth only in an actual life; an idea can be brought forth only in its intended medium—human existence.

Any reader is in a position of some sort to interpret Kierkegaard's writings for himself or herself. The characters Kierkegaard designed to carry his authorship enacted general types of existences: "The communication is an art in which the various pseudonyms do not simply talk about but exhibit the existential possibilities that make up their content" (Evans 1983, 106). The writings are attributed to some fictional person—Johannes de Silentio, Vigilius Haufniensis, Johannes Climacus—and even edited by fictional characters: Victor Eremita, Hilarius Bookbinder. They are situated in some definite point of view, which is not only depicted but often rendered problematical, as with the despair of the aesthete in the "Diapsalmata" of *Either/Or*. The pseudonymous writings develop stages or spheres of life that are based on general features of human existence. Readers, as human beings, have the capacity to entertain the depicted possibilities for themselves for potential reform: "They [human beings] are spatially and temporally located along with other physical realities, but they remember, they anticipate, they scheme, they fear, they fantacize: they ventilate their localized reality with myriad forms of possibility" (Crites 1972, 185). Kierkegaard believed that human reality was a becoming, a continual development, and he wrote for just such development through the process of self-examination. The "stages" are elusive and ambiguous, not definitive as expected. He communicates through existential movement, showing how a life might be projected into the real world through action. What the pseudonyms say is not necessarily what they mean, but what they portray is another matter:

> These modes of existence [Kierkegaard's characters] Kierkegaard conceives as universal and objective in content. However, what he desired to do was not merely to describe these modes of existence in an objective way; what he wished to do was to communicate them in such a way that his readers would consider them subjectively, that is, with an understanding that these are possibilities which confront them as individuals for rejection or actualization. (Evans 1978, 80)

One such character, Johannes Climacus, states:

> Existential reality is incommensurable, and the subjective thinker finds his reality in his own ethical existence. When reality is apprehended by an outsider, it can only be understood as possibility. Everyone who makes a communication . . . will therefore be careful to give his existential communication the form of possibility, precisely in order that it may have a relationship to existence. A communication in the form of possibility compels the recipient to face the problem of existing in it, insofar as this is possible between man and man. (Kierkegaard [1846] 1968, 105)

Johannes not only talks about this activity but also performs it as he prescribes it, exhibiting himself in his own works.

There are other characters: a seducer, a young man in love trying to relive what he once had, an "experimental psychologist," a judge, an actress reliving a part she had made famous as a young woman, a religious inquirer, a madman, women betrayed, a gallery of young men who live for the moment, a despairing and bitter aesthete, a religious devotee, and a variety of others. Some are more prominent in their modes of being in a world because they "author" books or essays; others are simply found in detailed descriptions. Yet each enacts some form of human possibility, and most readers will find a mirror to look into somewhere in Kierkegaard's works. He taps common human experience to provide realistically lived perspectives through which personal engagements are typically developed. "Each of them [the pseudonyms] is a synthesis of emotion, idea, disposition, will and plan" (Holmer 1981, 13).

Perhaps the most famous persona is the young seducer in *Either/ Or*. He patiently schemes and manipulates his way into a young woman's bed with elaborate ruses in order to convince her that the liaison is her idea. His description is in the form of day-to-day accounts of his activities and progress. The reader is presented, quite vividly, with an attitude in action—the diary of a man who plays out his ideas rather than just present them as a lecture, report, or thesis.

Kierkegaard uses hypothetical personalities, offering no results, and forces readers to come to their own conclusions: "This tentativeness creates the necessary distance between reader and author so that the reader grasps the truth for himself, if he grasps it at all" (Evans 1983, 106). The assumption behind the pseudonyms is that human beings have the capacity to grasp truth about and for themselves and, as such, can participate in human possibility when it is communicated to them indirectly through realistic but fictional enactment.

THE ROLE OF IMAGINATION

The particularities of human existence can be made intelligible for persons in their concrete situations via fictional portrayals that are, ostensibly, about "someone else." The artist shows us singularities. Shakespeare shows us Hamlet, not universal man; the character is presented in his unique and singular circumstances and is vividly intelligible to us as such. While one might say that Hamlet exemplifies a particular type of person, his individuality is also preserved.

Human possibility can be imaginatively relived by viewers of a dramatic conveyance like *Hamlet*. They can meet it with a personal response. In a similar way, Kierkegaard's fictive variations bear experiences and meaning that originate outside of limiting conceptual consciousness, and he is able to demand of his readers and to aid them in a transcendence of conceptual restrictions—to develop a state of mind by which they can resonate inwardly to images of their own actuality in the form of "possibility-for-me."

To vary the contexts of human possibility imaginatively is to be able to participate in the human community of meaning as it emerges from interactions and involvements with others. Imagination is the capacity to go beyond that which is immediately perceptible, to be able to make connections and disconnections. A vivid recreation of any idea allows the experience of emotion that might be associated with that idea to penetrate it. Evoking a response depends on the disposition of a mind toward such a response, and the person (i.e, the therapist) who wants to manipulate imagination for subjective communication must be attuned to a variety of such dispositions. Human beings respond rather undeliberately in their lived engagements, often experiencing that which is present to them by becoming like it. They grow quiet with quiet things, irritated with irritation, they mime smallness in the presence of smallness, they suffer with suffering. Imagination plays a dominant role in this response.

To imagine is to display relations in a depicting mode, channeling perception through a creative schematization. As Kant points out, imagination creates without mechanically following rules or methods; it aids in the completion of meaning. Imagination allows us to look into possibilities and grasp the actual. We grasp what actually *is* only after we have grasped what might be. To see ourselves is, in part, to be able to imaginatively set before ourselves an array of possible ways of being and to detect our own among the many. Absence—that of which we are habitually unaware—can thus be called into presence—into our awareness—through artifice and fiction. By contributing to the bracketing of ordinary reference, imagination contributes to the projection of new possibilities for self-involvement. The self can see things about itself that had before been hidden. Imagination can allow outside possibilities to sting individuals into looking where habitual patterns typically blind them.

Don Ihde (1977) points out that seeing something in a new way disturbs the original way it was seen, loosening the strength of the original conative grip. The first way of seeing is then restructured for the person as just one of several possibilities. For example, if Diane is able to see her self-induced emotional paralysis as only one of many possible available alternatives, rather than as necessary reality for herself, she is freed to make choices about what she is doing and what she might do. She can continue as she is, make alterations, or entirely replace her old modes with new ones. The use of imagination allows indirect communicational structures that promote a human exchange that entails more than directly expressible understanding; it has the power to penetrate a life and to evoke a realization of one's own style of experiencing. Utilizing meaning structures in therapy to disturb the habitual experiencing of the client is an effective means of communicating to the client *how* he or she is experiencing.

Further Comments on Indirect Communication

It must be noted that direct and indirect communication are not to be construed as explicit and implicit forms of expression. Explicit expression can serve as a sign to a hidden (implicit) meaning, but both the sign and the meaning are still objects for reflection. Both *can* be put into words. For example, the sorts of implications that H. P. Grice (1961) draws out in his discussion of the causal theory of reference may be misunderstood as indirect communication because they are a "hidden" communication. Some unspoken message can be implied through what speakers assert; through their manner of speaking (their saying *that* in that way or their not saying something that seems obviously present in its absence), and through the words that are actually used. For example, a letter of recommendation for a candidate for a position in philosophy that states only that Jones has beautiful handwriting and good grammar implies that he is no good at philosophy. What the speaker did not say is the vehicle for this implication. Although the implication is not directly expressed, it is, in principle, directly expressible. However, that such implication is possible points to the further possibility of a communication that is, in principle, *not* directly expressible. That we can understand another's message without having them speak it directly indicates that we also may be able to apprehend "messages" that cannot be spoken, but that can be implied in a person's style or being in the world. Indirect communication is not equivalent to *what* can be inferred but to *how* the inference strikes one. It is not a simple utilization of unexpressed concepts, nor is it composed of tacit assertions. It is the medium for communicating the experiencing of an individual that preserves it *and protects it* from the mediation of linguistically expressed concepts.

Nor is indirect communication to be misconstrued as nonverbal communication, which is also an objectifiable process. Postures, gestures, facial expressions, voice inflections, and all other clues present to an observer are objective. The subjectivity of an individual can be apprehended to some degree by these clues, but, once again, indirect communication relates to the intuitively grasped *how* and not to the *what* of an individual's existence.

In therapy, indirect communication can be an important tool, both for reminding the therapist of the subjective dimensions of human experiencing and for accessing the subjectivity of the clients and communicating back to them what is detected. A variety of techniques for such indirection are applicable in therapy, and the following chapter details a number of them specifically for and in a therapeutic setting.

5
Applications to Therapy

The Merging of the "How" and "What"

Indirect communication enables the therapist to be aware of and to explore much more of the clinical dynamic than exclusive attention to verbally explicit objective content allows. As clinicians explore beyond what can be said or observed, they will develop a sense of the integral relations of the "how" and the "what" of the client's presence in the therapeutic exchange. They will have taken the first step in the process of dealing with the client as an experiencing person. They will have more access to the experiential processes that objective formulation eclipses. If therapists attend both to the content of their clients' experience and to the subjective style in which clients relate themselves to their world, an importantly unified dialectic will emerge.

Therapists desire to be as effective as they can. They may suppose that a detailed objective system will give them more in this regard, even at the expense of missing some features of the situation. Yet they do an injustice to the client, who desires to be regarded as a full human being. They also miss essential features of a person's lived involvement in his or her situation. Without abandoning objective methods, indirect communication simply goes beyond them to penetrate more of the client's presence. Clinging to a categorized system sacrifices too much. Fully verbalized concepts and diagnoses fail to show the client to either the therapist or to the client. Instead, it provokes an intrapersonal fragmentation in both.

Therapists need to attend to the experiencing as a factor in the experienced; they must see that any distinctions that separate the two aspects of being human are artificially imposed, often to serve prejudices of the scientific community. *All* aspects of the phenomena should be allowed into the therapeutic matrix undistorted. Although the "objective" and "subjective" are, on some level, mutually exclusive, they are also mutually necessary for knowledge of human existence—as they are present both in the knower and in the human being who is the focus of the knower's inquiry. The "how" and "what" together compose all phenomena about what it is to be human, not as separable and independent parts, but in a dialectically indistinguishable blend.

Although a growing number of therapists have tried to develop more poetic, imagistic approaches to the clinical dynamic, Kierkegaard makes a special contribution with his emphasis on subjectivity and double reflection. All clinical observations must be informed through a human sensitivity grounded in the self-awareness of the therapist. Only then can the client's personality unfold in its rich spectrum of cognitive-emotional structures. The clinician, then, must be both observer and observed.

Not through analytic acknowledgement but through a double reflection—an awareness of one's presence in one's activities—will therapists be enabled to keep their own humanity in mind, to perceive how their personal perspective infiltrates their interventions. As an observer of human experience, therapists must identify themselves closely with the "observed other." "Observation," says Kierkegaard, "is not a receiving but a creation, and the decisive factor is *how* the observer is" ([1843] 1971, 67). Therapists concerned about their clients must begin by being concerned with themselves. He or she must be an "observing I" as well as an "observed-I-in-the-other." That is, therapists should experience something of themselves in both positions. Only then will they be prepared for the highly artistic process of indirect communication, which relies on the wholistic blend of subjectivity with objectivity.

An examination of some of what therapists have done to facilitate indirect communication will further reveal how Kierkegaard's detailed analysis of the human condition helps make indirect communication possible.

Applications

Before indirect communication can be utilized in therapy, therapists must acknowledge the full range of subjective influence, not only within the client, but within themselves. They must look to their own perspectives, biases, blindnesses, and so forth, in order to see how *they* influence the course of therapy. In turn, they must recognize the experiential flow of their clients from which beliefs, behaviors, and attitudes emerge.

In May's *Existence* (1958), Binswanger details the cases of Ellen West and of Ilse to show insanity and neurosis as "life-historical" phenomena. He gives facts about age, religion, family, education, and so on; he also discusses the histories of the cases, as well as much of the developments in therapy for each of these women.

Ilse is self-abusive and suicidal. Things she says and does and situations in which she makes discoveries reveal that the theme of "love for her father" runs throughout her actions; she claims that her self-abuse is a sacrificial act for him. Binswanger includes his sense of Ilse's situation in a lengthy discussion, showing his own theoretical understanding as her world opens out to him. One can trace the dialectic between therapist and client in both of these cases because Binswanger gives enough detail to show something of the matrix (subject/object, subject/subject, object/object) as it developed between them. One can also gain a sense of the client's style of being in the world as it folds into Binswanger's clinical descriptions.

These two cases were among the first to be presented through an existential framework, which called for subjectivity to be regarded as a significant feature of the clinical situation. Binswanger allows the world of his clients to stand out to him in their fully lived qualities.

Individuals like Ilse, and like Diane from the previous chapter, are involved in lived engagements with the things they know. "How" they participate in "what" they know is integral to a formulation of the concepts of their knowledge. They have a way of knowing that is not limited to true/false propositions but that is generated in their actual involvement in what they know.

Therapy is further complicated by the interaction of two such individuals, like Binswanger with Ilse, both of whom live in the tension of the objective/subjective dialectic. Concentration on only the objective part of this exchange generates only a partial understanding. Similarly, concentration on only one of the participants robs the dynamic of some of its power as well as shuts out influences at play in the exchange. A partial understanding is a distortion of what has actually taken place between the two participants. Therapy needs an understanding of the entire exchange in all of its features to be therapeutic to the whole person. Diane's case shows how this works.

When Diane smoked and giggled her way through a task that seemed to make her nervous, then denied that she had done so, she indicated to her therapist that she was partially alienated from herself. She had disavowed significant aspects of her reactions to family relations, particularly toward her mother. She did not perceive the evidence of her tension, but the therapist did. When he drew her attention explicitly to what he had noted, she persisted in remaining ignorant of it. A gap in her sense of herself was evident to him. He assumed that she had reasons for keeping areas of her life apart from her awareness—reasons that she might be unaware of; her reasons were evidently strong enough to produce an absentmindedness about her self-fragmenting.

The therapist, through a sympathetic bond via shared common humanity, perceived Diane's tensions through behaviors characteristic of tension. He noticed this because he was open to his own tensions. Yet, she did not affirm his interpretation. A second level of experiencing became evident to him through her denials. He called on his own experience to understand what Diane was showing through her puzzling denial.

The therapist, in graduate school, had once been confronted with his own form of self-deception. In a group practicum situation with other counseling students, he had resisted what the others wanted to do, claiming that he did not really care what went on in the group. When one group member persisted in trying to draw him in, he shouted out, "I don't care!" The other man sat for a moment, then shouted back, "I don't care!" The mimicry was effective. The therapist had spotted the emotional way in which he had denied having any emotions. He knew then that it was possible to be blind to oneself, and he knew experientially what it was like.

Aware that not all engagements in which an individual participates are explicitly present to that individual, the therapist was able to relate to Diane's world. She had closed herself off, then had developed automatic habits that engulfed her in and perpetuated her self-obscuring. She was able to achieve this state by preventing her acts of disavowal from becoming explicit to her. The therapist, having recognized the same thing in himself, could understand more easily how Diane could act without being aware of her activity.

Diane's *refusal* to be aware of aspects of her attitudes and behaviors transforms tacit engagements into blocked ones. In the same way that making something explicit often involves reasons for doing so, the therapist can infer that *avoiding* such activity stems from some reason as well. To gain a deeper sense of this possibility, he can view it as a possibility for himself. By thus regarding it, he can realize it in Diane by understanding what it might be like for him if he did not want to know something about himself (and thereby remembering what it *was* like). His own clinical training had shown him such blindspots in himself, making explicit just how they had become blindspots for him. His own avoidance of these areas had been not just a denial of them, but a way of sealing them off from his conscious awareness, to guard against having them pointed out to him. No outsider could tell him that he in fact felt very strongly

about the group activities; he alone had been in control of what he
would or would not make explicit to himself about himself. It was
his choice to preserve the power to reflect over his experiencing or
to undermine that power. Thus, he knew that he could conceal engagements from himself so that even the concealing is concealed.

Self-deception is an intentional ignorance through which one can
stubbornly remain "in ignorance" (Fingarette 1969). Persons may
have a vague sense of what they are doing but so position themselves that they cannot acknowledge that sense. Their deferred engagement is kept nonthematic and is thus isolated from everything
that is—or that potentially is—made explicit. The ambiguous nature of the self, with its tacit areas of lived immediacy, allows such a
puzzling but pervasive activity.

Thus, the therapist's own experiencing allowed him a sense of
what Diane might be doing. His inference was formed through a
self-reflective response to her. From his own experience of being
surprised in his experiential fragmenting, he can see hers more
clearly; that is, through his own double reflection, he was able to see
more of her experiencing than she did, because a double reflection is
blocked on her part. While her behaviors were present to him objectively on the level of observation, his understanding of her was a
subjectively formed reflection. *What* he thought about her was
permeated by his own experience-informed relation to what he
thinks.

Without a sense of his own human experiencing and its possibilities, he would have been left with nothing more than an objective
contradiction: She does A but denies doing A. In addition, he would
be limited to a direct approach back to her, simply telling her that
she does A and denies doing A. Neither result would be very productive. To tell someone that she is under an illusion about herself
might not dispel the illusion; it might further alienate her both from
herself and from the therapist. She might retreat further into the
illusion. That Diane, in her reflective state, denies what she appears
to be experiencing indicates that she is cognitively separated from
herself. Further reflection that might make her an object for herself
would hardly draw her closer to her own experiencing. She must be
shown "how" she is, and she can only be shown this through non-
refential, indirect means. Kierkegaard offered an analogy that suits
this situation: "When a man has his mouth so full of food that he is
prevented from eating, and is like to starve in consequence, does
giving him food consist in stuffing still more of it in his mouth, or
does it consist in taking some of it away, so that he can begin to eat?"
([1846] 1968, 245). A direct communication to a person who rejects

it requires gentle handling. Diane has an "objective knowledge" about herself, even though it is inaccurate; she knows that she suffers from daily nausea, that she has problems with her boyfriend, that she doesn't want to pick up the phone when it rings. More "knowledge" of this form is like stuffing more food into a full mouth. To be shown *how* she is, she must be caught off-guard so that her control over her complex of disavowals is momentarily lost. The resulting gap between herself and her control may allow her a glimpse of that which she has refused to see.

Why she has refused to face something about herself is not as much an issue in the communication to her of herself as is the *means* by which she will be able to face what she has refused to face. If the communication successfully shows her to herself, she will know enough about the "why" to do something about what is brought to her awareness. Or if she does not, she will at least have more information to work this out with the therapist. His detective work will be reduced in either case.

It is possible, of course, for the therapist to be wrong. His own hermeneutical position is limited, but he is trained to see more about people than they see of themselves and his training would give him confidence to pursue his initial intuitions until they ultimately fail to check out. However, he has some support (overt behaviors, cigarette butts) in the "objective" evidence.

Diane giggled, erased, and smoked in such a manner that the therapist inferred tension and nervousness. Had he never been nervous or tense, he might not have been able to interpret this evidence about Diane. What he infers depends in large degree on how he infers—how much he has available to him through his own experiential repertoire. He may not have been correct, but his own human experiencing allowed him a mimetic attunement to Diane that made him somewhat confident of his assertions even in the face of her vehement denial.

This is not to say that Diane's therapist can only be effective if he has experienced everything experienced by her (or any other client). Rather, an awareness of his own subjective modes directs his attention to the subjectivity of outwardly evident behaviors and expressions. *How* he has been in his own self-awareness cues him into something of how others might be in their own self-awareness. There is no one-to-one correlation of experiencing with experiencing, but shared humanity serves as a meeting ground between two or more people such that each can be aware of the other(s) as being like them, and the perceived similarity of their experiencing can allow them to consider as "possibility-for-me" what they

apprehend in others. That is, although the therapist may not have
tense family relations, he has been in tension-provoking situations
and can recognize tension when it is enacted in some way by a client
like Diane. He can make conjectures about the subjectivity of
another person that are informed by his own.

In short, the indirect communication works like this, with "A"
representing the therapist and "B" the client: A observes a behavior
or attitude in B that indicates that B is involved in self-deception. A
recognizes this through what he knows via training and his own experience (the "observed-I-in-the-other"). B's behavior may have
provoked a visceral response in him, getting him to double-reflect
his thinking back to his lived manner and history (the "observed-
I"). A wants to provoke B to "reengage" with herself. A needs a
device to show B to herself. If A has not yet double-reflected when
thinking about B, he must do so in order to devise a means of provoking double-reflection in B; he must use a device that will be isomorphic in structure to B's situation—a mirror. A may tell B a story
in which a character is in B's situation, acting as B acts. B will only
see the similarity through a double-reflection. If she does, communication has been achieved, indirectly via a bond of inarticulate
common experiencing between A and B.

The subjective and the objective are essentially integrated, then,
through both the positive results of their dialectic and the negative
results of their separation. For the therapist, *what* he reflects over,
what he perceives as he attends to Diane is informed through his
mimetic human involvement. His own relation to his thinking expands the objective content of his thought; it becomes a product of a
subjectively involved reflection. His knowledge of Diane grows
beyond that which can be contained in verbal diagnosis, theory, and
treatment because his inarticulate experiencing is tapped for a significant contribution. He recognizes that he is not observing inanimate
nature but a human being in process of experiencing her world. And
because *he* is human, he has a sense of that process and that it can
never be completely objectifiable from either a first- or third-person
point of view.

On the other hand, Diane's sense of *herself*, at least in the area in
which she is having difficulty, is *un*integrated. *What* she "knows" is
cut off from her immediate engagements. Her consciousness is fragmented, the pieces isolated from one another. When she is told that
she is not aware of everything she is doing, she can only assess that
information without the benefits of a full experiential verification;
she is thus prone to rejecting a truth about herself because she cannot draw it into her lived awareness. She is reflectively separated

from this area of her experiencing and cannot gain a fully lived view of herself.

Individuals cannot have a full self-awareness without both objective reflection and subjective reflection. *What* we know is inevitably integrated with *how* we know. The first reflection cannot be cut off from experiencing because every reflection involves a background flow of experiencing that is not brought into conscious view. The immediacy of one's own most personal style of experiencing tends to be kept within one's shadow—and this, perversely enough, happens sometimes *because* of one's attempts to reflect on it! We may attempt to gain distance on ourselves through the first reflection, but we carry our subjectivity *with* us as we step back. Subjective reflection alone has no objective content to relate to. *How* individuals experience a *what* allows them a sense of their own attunement to that "what," to know if it is true for them—that is, if it is right, full, harmonious for them. Yet they do not have a full sense of their experiencing of it without the reflective content. We need both for a full apprehension of ourselves.

The indirect approach is more artistic than scientific, being intuitive rather than empirical. It depends not on regularities, causal sequences, and strict observation, but on the development of a skill that is tested and developed with each case. It is founded on the recognition that, although human beings may leave trails behind them that can become objects for study, the individual determines the trail in his or her own way. The therapist must realize that the "trail" is only part of the story.

If objective evidence were all that was needed for therapy, therapists would have to memorize an overwhelming amount of information on behaviors and expressions that correlates with lived experiencing; they would also need some means by which to distinguish between behaviors that correspond to more than one mode of engagement. Where would such information be gathered? It would have to be formulated by speculative abstraction alone, but there is more to human existence than abstraction can account for. In addition, human experiencing in both the "human object" and in the speculator is much too ambiguous for the precise delineations required to catalogue all human behaviors, gestures, and outward expressions. We cannot get away from the fact that understanding *how* an individual is engaged in the world is essential to understanding human existence, both for the theorist and for the person interestedly engaged in his or her world. Kierkegaard points to double reflection and mimetic identification, by which one can avoid the "catalogue" approach.

Therapy is not learned by rote but is an activity that involves at least two existing individuals who are actively engaged in the process. And if therapy is human activity, the communication of it must be more than a parrotlike echo—a passing on of "results." The participants ask and answer questions in actual existence and truth is appropriated by drawing it through their experiencing.

That Diane denied what is evident to the therapist is an act that is drawn through the therapist's own experiencing of both her and himself. As he gains some sense of Diane's apparent inconsistency, he must find a way to show it to her that will not force her further into her illusions. As Kierkegaard perceptively points out, "one must approach from behind the person who is under an illusion" ([1847] 1962, 24–25). Diane must be moved to appropriate his insights on a level in which *what* he knows will be translated into *how* she is—the level at which she is experiencing. If the therapist is correct about her, and if he develops the appropriate form of communication with her, he should be able to strike a chord in her, much like a successful actor provokes a response from an audience. If he is wrong or clumsy in his communication, she will not respond. To be effective, the therapist must develop skills in discernment and in meaningful communication.

By preserving the lived immediacy of experiencing in his communication with her, the therapist can direct Diane's attention to her lived engagements by provoking a double reflection in her in spite of herself. He keeps the possible and the actual working together by utilizing a dialectic between the content of her situation and his experiencing of his own realities to formulate a subjectively informed content of possibility-for-her. Thus, what he presents and how he presents it allows an appropriation by another individual with commonly shared experience.

Techniques of Indirect Communication

Before discussing four techniques through which indirect communication can be achieved, a word must be said about the context for utilizing metaphorical messages. While some of the following examples are dramatic, and seem not to do justice to the fully involved therapeutic situation, it must be noted that responsible therapists do not use mirroring without forethought. Therapists spend a great deal of time learning about their clients, trying to decide what will work best with a given individual. Different people have different communication styles. With some clients, straightforward verbal communication is effective and therefore sufficient. Others overintellectualize. Still others, like Diane and Paul, seem resistant to a straight verbal diagnosis. Others fall naturally into indirect communication themselves, describing their symptoms and situations metaphorically. Therapists must get to know their clients before determining their approach. They must establish rapport and discern patterns. Indirect communication is neither easy nor quick, contrary to how it may seem in the necessary brevity of some of the examples. At times it works surprisingly well, and these are the examples most commonly reported. At other times, it may take a number of attempts from various angles before something works, and then may only work slightly. The cases reported have extensive backgrounds and follow-up.

Indirect messages, whether they are verbal or enacted through a role, contain ambiguous meanings; referents are undefined. There may even be contradictions. The interpretation becomes a matter of the hermeneutical position of the recipients of such communication. They must think more deeply than usual to make sense of it. Indeed, their ordinary manner of reflecting may have to be disrupted.

IRONY

The most simple and obvious form of indirect communication is irony. Irony stings the person targeted, alerting him or her to actions and/or styles of acting. When we meet a person who broke his leg tripping over a log and we comment about his gracefulness, we practice irony. A double reflection almost inevitably occurs as the inappropriateness of the literal communication forces another interpretation, in which the person must see the reason for the remark. Kierkegaard utilized and analyzed this form of communication. However, irony is not a common tool for therapy.

PARADOX

Something close to irony but more therapeutic is the use of paradox. Clients are treated in such a way that they conclude that they are expected to change by remaining unchanged. Their very symptoms are prescribed for them, placing them in a double bind. If they comply, they no longer "cannot help it"; they do it. If they resist, they no longer act out their symptoms. They gain control through either elimination or through voluntary intentional action. They are forced to see their frame of reference for their debilitating activities. New perspectives are created: "The therapeutic double bind implicitly challenges the client's model of the world by forcing him/her into an experience which contradicts the self-destructive limitations of the present model" (Weeks and L'Abate 1982, 7). This double bind is brought about through mimicry, exaggeration, irony, ridicule, distortion, humor, or sarcasm. Clients are stung into the awareness that their beliefs about themselves *are* theirs, and that such beliefs comprise only one possible way to think about themselves.

Alfred Adler was the first person to use and write about these techniques. He first gave the client "permission" to have the symptom, then predicted its return. He would exaggerate the symptom or take it more seriously than did the client. He would redefine it in some positive way, and then prescribe the symptom as the avenue for change, asking the client to refine and improve it as much as possible.

Paradoxical psychotherapy is utilized by other therapists as well. Weeks and L'Abate report a case in which a client claimed that everyone hated her. She declared that she should just go off and live in the woods. The therapist asked her to write down a list of things that others had done to reveal how they hated her. She was able to list only twenty-four items. The therapist told her the list was unconvincing; other clients had provided him with twice as much and more, yet were not as upset as she. However, the therapist did agree that "something was going on." He also agreed that living in the woods alone would be "the safest thing for her." The therapist's words placed the problem in perspective. The woman saw that she had been acting childishly and went on to discuss what was really troubling her (Weeks and L'Abate 1982, 138).

This client "saw" herself in the paradoxical twist where the therapist took her more seriously than she did herself. The sort of neurosis that is a (hidden) self-mockery can emerge as such for the patient when the therapist takes it very seriously; that is, the therapist mocks the patient, whose self-mockery is revealed through the therapist's.

A more forceful example involves Eddie, a 39-year-old male who was transferred after nineteen years from a state hospital to a community home. At the home, Eddie refused to cooperate with house procedure. He acted helpless, staying in bed most of the time, and whined when he was up. He felt he had "done everything in life there is to do."

Therapists agreed with Eddie that he had, indeed, done everything, and the only thing left was to prepare to die.

> We took Eddie's door off the hinges, brought it down to the living room. . . . Now Eddie was to lie in state dressed in his best suit, holding rosary beads. . . .

We informed everyone in the house that Eddie was "basically dead," and that we were waiting for his soul to leave his body. (Bergman 1982, 219–20)

When this form of therapeutic intervention was introduced, Eddie jumped up and screamed that he was not dead. The therapists "reframed" this as a "death cackle." Eddie lay "in state" for three days, while the other residents viewed his body and referred to him in the past tense.

"On the fourth morning, a miracle happened. Eddie started going to the Day Program, refused to sleep or stay in his room for more than seven hours, began to date women . . ." (Bergman 1982, 220). Eddie had seen himself as others saw him; the reality of the crazy thing he was doing to himself finally dawned on him and he decided to change, although the change itself was gradual.

Although Kierkegaard never mentioned paradox specifically, his ideas about indirect communication still apply. When clients are faced with contradiction, they are forced to figure out what they must do. They must "untie the complex knot" for themselves. They expect one thing, they get another. This situation is consistent with Kierkegaard's belief that human existence possesses contradictions that throw individuals on their own resources, provoking the inward reflection of lived awareness evident in both cases above.

ROLE-PLAYING

Enacting a role often helps to communicate the self-as-lived back to the self. A role condenses and thematizes an individual's style, making explicit that which is ordinarily implicit. As pointed out earlier, a role is a physiognomic metaphor, revealing on the surface the feelings within: patterns are lifted out of lived situations, soaking the concrete particularities into themselves. A role can stand in for lived experiencing because it can closely resemble the experiencing; it can affect a person just as the actual experiencing might.

The most common type of role-playing is where one person plays another. Diane's therapist had experienced the effects of role-playing when the other group member portrayed him in his anger. The role, played by another, recreated him. The experience affected him as a direct communication could not. He had been told that he was angry and emotional by some of the other group members, but his own self-denying absorption had prevented him from acknowledging this. Instead, he had clung more firmly to his denials. Watching himself reenacted brought home to him what he had failed to comprehend through a direct verbal communication.

A role might also be played by the same person whom it recreates. Paul (the timid adolescent from chapter 3) might be asked to play himself coming into a room. By doing so, he might be alerted to habitual modes that echo, viscerally, the patterns of self-belittlement that he had denied. Seeing himself doing it might be more effective than being told that he is doing it.

The therapist might also play an effective role as a mirror. Philip Barker (1985) offers an impressive example of a therapist playing a role of self-questioner in order to provoke the members of a family into seeing how the questions that he posed to himself could also be posed by each of them to themselves.

There were five members of the Evans family, each of whom had attended four earlier therapy sessions. Their "family complaint" centered on John, 14, who had developed some serious behavioral problems. John had improved over the four sessions. When the family showed up for its fifth session, the father was absent.

The therapist felt that Mr. Evans had been rather uninvolved, both emotionally and physically, with the other members of the family, possibly because he felt little warmth or caring from them. He was usually busy with his work. With John's problems, the father had become more involved, but now was slipping back into former habits.

Mrs. Evans informed the therapist that Mr. Evans would no longer be attending the sessions. The therapist decided that the father's absence needed to be dealt with, but to raise the issue was tricky. He did not wish to imply or state criticism of Mr. Evans to the other family members. He also did not wish to lay blame on anyone. So he used a more subtle approach:

> At the start of the session the therapist asked all the four members present, in turn, what they thought the therapist might have done in the last session . . . that had contributed to Mr. Evans' non-attendance to-day. Had he said something tactless to him? Had he made him feel left out of the discussion? Had he shown him insufficient care and concern? Not enough warmth and acceptance, perhaps? Did the father feel in some way blamed for the family's problems? . . . How did the therapist manage to leave Mr. Evans, apparently, with the idea that treatment could proceed satisfactorily without him? What could the therapist do now that would help the father once again become part of the therapy process? (25–26)

As Barker points out, the questions had a metaphorical twist. Each question gave family members the opportunity to wonder what had upset the father, and whether any of them was somehow involved in his absence. "Almost inevitably, the other family members would find themselves thinking about things *they* might have done or said to Mr. Evans that could have upset him or played a part in causing him to withdraw from the family" (26). In addition, the questioning process about the family involvement in therapy was a metaphor for other family activities from which Mr. Evans had withdrawn.

Other types of role-playing have equal potential for affecting changes in a situation or relationship. Papp (1982) uses "couples choreography" to reframe marital relationships in metaphorical ways, such as as a tug of war contest. It is similar to "family sculpting" (Papp 1980, Barker 1985). One family member is appointed as the "sculptor," whose task is to place the other members into positions that he or she feels represent the interactions that take place. Everyone can observe, quite vividly, how that family member feels about the way the rest of the family relates to one another. For example, if a child is worried about the way his parents fight all the time, he might set them into boxing positions, or—with a view to a frighteningly possible future—he might put them in separate rooms from one another. In one "sculpted" family, the children were all placed with their backs to each other, facing in different directions. The mother was posed in a position of pulling them along behind her (with great difficulty), and the father stood some distance away, watching with an indifferent expression—as he put it, "from the peanut gallery." If each family member "choreographs" the family interactions from his or her point of view, the similarities and dissimilarities can be strikingly evocative for therapeutic discussion. In addition, family members might be requested by the therapist to "sculpt" how they think the family should be, and then to make appropriate comparisons. While this sort of activity is typically construed as "nonverbal" rather than "indirect" therapy, it has the potential to provoke double reflection, and thus to facilitate indirect communication.

Other physiognomic metaphors involve not so much role-playing as using an object that shows something more than direct expression might effect. For example, a therapist drew out an awareness in his clients that would probably have been overlooked if he had not acted as he did: "One young couple had reached an impasse. They were vague about their complaints and maintained emotional distance in their relationship. The partners were sitting on opposite ends of a sofa in a session when the therapist began to place bean bag chairs between them" (Gordon 1978, 89). Through this physical metaphor, they recognized how they had distanced themselves from one another. The beanbag chair played the "role" of emotional distance via physical space.

Whether role-playing is done with people, objects, or positions, the main point is that the role-playing technique be isomorphic to that for which it stands in. Recognizing oneself when stung by similarity catches people off their reflective guard long enough to provoke the double reflection that relates them immediately to their own lived engagements.

Metaphorical performance is effective because it probes more deeply within the individual than general description can; its pattern can be made-to-order for the concrete realities of personal uniqueness. No general rules for interpretation apply and the individual must respond from within his or her own lived experiencing: "understanding a metaphor is as much a creative endeavor as making a metaphor, and as little guided by rules" (Davidson 1981, 200). Meaning is coconstituted by the creator and the interpreter.

Many therapists who actively utilize role-playing in the course of therapy are influenced by Milton Erickson, whose theory of indirect communication was outlined in chapter 3. Erickson and Kierkegaard are in close agreement. For both thinkers, images played an important part. Both relied on imagistically structured devices that forced the client—for Erickson—or the reader—for Kierkegaard— toward his or her basic human experiencing: images were used that had the power to provoke a double reflection (although Erickson did not use this terminology). Kierkegaard's character portrayals are similar to role-playing techniques in that he attempted to help readers locate themselves in other "people." Erickson's teaching tales (such as the story of his father) accomplished a similar goal.

However, one of the therapies in which role-playing is most popular is Gestalt Therapy, which does not share (at least superficially) Kierkegaard's analysis. In Gestalt Therapy, meaning is a relation of figure to background. A "gestalt" is organized by the weighting of needs for an individual. A healthy individual experiences free flow from figure to background. An unmet or blocked need makes a rigid gestalt. When a need is met, the individual no longer saps his or her organismic energy.

To meet their needs, people must develop a sharpened sensory awareness with which to identify (or "own") who they are, as well as an aggressiveness to get what they need. They need to be in vigilant contact with important events in their environment/organism configuration. The emphasis is on seeing and feeling, in the present.

Unlike with Kierkegaard, the focus for Gestalt Therapy is on the figure. Background is acknowledged as a necessary part of the gestalt, but nothing is said about the double reflection that relates one to the other. Gestalt Therapy is more objectively oriented and more directive than is typical with indirect communication: "tell me what you feel"; "what are you aware of now?"

However, gestalt as theory is related to phenomenology, a philosophy that acknowledges Kierkegaard's perceptive analysis of subjectivity, and that, like Kierkegaard, attempts to hold systematic theory and interpretation at arm's length. This gives Gestalt Therapy more in common with Kierkegaard, at the outset, than at first might seem to be the case.

In addition, the move toward a figure/background configuration acknowledges the living flow of experiencing in a manner not so far removed from what Kierkegaard points to. While there may be some significant points of theoretical separation, it would not distort some of the implicit assumptions involved in Gestalt Therapy to say that they could have much of their grounding in Kierkegaard's analysis of human existence. But Kierkegaard goes beyond Gestalt Therapy, as he does with Erickson and his colleagues, by detailing the involvement of subjectivity and by developing a sense of the double reflection that brings us viscerally to ourselves.

VERBAL METAPHORS

A verbal metaphor consists of stories, allegories, parables, similies, sentences, or descriptions. The function of a linguistic metaphor is to extend language, to say what cannot be said in literal terms alone. It increases the depth and finesse of communication, calling attention to otherwise undesignated aspects of human existence: "Metaphor plugs the gaps in literal vocabulary" (Black 1981, 69). We often find that recourse to metaphor is the only way to convey something to another person: " My arm feels like a lead weight"; "It was like waking up to springtime!" Metaphor puts a new sense on words that we use. In short, the verbal metaphor is a collection of implications for selecting, emphasizing, and/or organizing relations in human reality.

The indirect communicator can use verbal metaphor to sum up themes that have been kept implicit in the life of another; he or she can use any of the various devices listed above to stand in for parts of the other's experiencing. Therapists often resort to one of these devices when trying to get their clients to see something that is not easily put into words.

Taking their cue from the way practiced storytellers get their listeners to *live* inside of themselves the adventures told, therapists of the Neurolinguistic Programming tradition (Bandler and Grinder 1979) utilize metaphors to convey nonlinguistic messages: "*Some-*

one is confronted with *some* problem which he/she overcomes (or succumbs to) in some way. The way in which the protagonist resolves the problem can provide a possible solution for others in a similar bind" (Gordon 1978, 7). Verbal metaphor operates much like the physiognomic metaphors of theatre. A story becomes significant to people familiar with its content in virtue of their own experiencing. It makes them curious about the story's resolution; they are open to it even if they block similar resolutions that have been more straightforwardly delivered to them. The story, poem, fable, parable, joke, and so forth, *speak* to the person in a way that direct expression cannot. The person's lived engagement is expressed in terms of something else similar to it such that new light is shed on a situation. Metaphor is representable to that person through his or her own experiencing.

The therapist must gain as much understanding as possible of the client's experiencing. Metaphors aid both in the gathering of information about clients and in therapeutic intervention. For example, a therapist might ask a client to tell a story, or to complete a story from a picture or from an opening statement such as "Jack was a man with a problem." What the client does with such an ambiguously structured device may yield important themes. Metaphorical expression provides a mutually comprehensible way of relating to the client's situation without mediating it through direct description; it preserves the structure of the client's situation: "the significant factors in the metaphor are the client's interpersonal relationships and patterns of coping within the context of the 'problem'" (Gordon 1978, 119). It goes further, however, in that it can also provide a solution.

David Gordon gives the example of Joe, who is having problems with his wife—she takes little initiative because he insists on taking most of the responsibility for care of the family. She "mopes" around the house and he is at a loss as to what to do about her. Most of the therapy sessions revolve around his difficulty understanding her, his loneliness, and his frustrations in trying to motivate her. The therapist, realizing after futile attempts that Joe is not a person to whom one can simply say, "You're contributing to the problem," tells Joe a metaphorical anecdote about a "friend of his in college." Accordingly, the "friend" was skilled at writing lab reports for science courses. His girlfriend was a science major too, and they shared many projects and assignments, including the lab reports.

There was one problem, however. The girlfriend felt rather incompetent when it came to writing the reports, so she sat back and let the fellow do it all. He was satisfied with this arrangement for awhile, but soon grew tired of doing all the work. He also thought she needed to try out her own skills. He thought up a way to get her involved.

One day he pretended that he was unable to write the report. The girlfriend filled in the words he needed. He thanked her, but was soon "stumped " again. She helped again, and it continued like this until she was writing whole sections of the report herself. "The next time they did a lab," said the therapist, "she actually demanded her fair share of it, and he was, of course, happy to share it with her" (Gordon 1978, 19).

The anecdote parallels Joe's situation and speaks to him through its similarity, although in a nonthreatening way so that he can attend to it unguarded. The therapist used the anecdote so that Joe could correlate it, consciously or unconsciously, to his own experience and possibly see the solution that is available to him. Above all, it shows him that there *is* a solution. The patterns that characterize Joe's problem are preserved in the structure of the story. Once identified, Joe can utilize what the story offers him in his own way. Only Joe can come home to Joe.

Another example of a verbal metaphor involves a woman who stayed with a husband who continually abused her. Time and again she came to therapy with injuries, yet did not see how leaving her husband would help matters. The therapist saw the futility of her situation more clearly than she did, but was unable to convince her. He told her the following story:

> The story was about a man who worked in a saw mill. The man was in one part of the mill stacking some freshly cut boards when he suddenly heard a terrible cry from the other room. He immediately rushed in to investigate and came across one of his co-workers standing by an enormous circular saw. The co-worker was clutching his hand in great pain, and had obviously just severed a finger from his left hand. The man who had just entered ran up to him exclaiming, "Oh my God, what happened?" To which the other responded, "Well I was just reaching for that board like this and . . . OUCH! THERE GOES ANOTHER ONE!" (Dilts 1980, 44).

The woman listened attentively to the story. It was clear to the therapist that she had been affected by it at a level he had been unable to reach any other way. She told him that she perceived similarities between the man in the story and herself. She was being just as foolish as the man who reached back into the saw. It was not long before she left her husband and started a life of her own in another town. As she told her therapist, she "didn't want to cut off another finger." While more dramatic than most results with indirect communication, this story does reveal the potential power of such a technique.

Milton Erickson used another kind of metaphor in his therapy. While verbal, it also provoked a great deal of imagery that had deliberate similarities to the situation of a given client: "He gave each spouse in a conflictual relationship a symbolic task. One was to climb a mountain while the other visited an arboretum. Then they switched tasks. The tasks gave each an opportunity to recognize their typical patterns of behavior" (Gordon 1978, 142). When each saw what the other did with a task that they had just imaginatively performed, it often provided an insight into the individual's particular way of doing things. From there they were able to discuss possible changes and to work on motivation for marital harmony.

Symbolism is an essential part of the "guided fantasy," another verbal metaphorical technique. This is a structured exercise that is basically empty of content, similar to Erickson's tasks outlined earlier. The basic direction for a fantasy is suggested to an individual and the individual's manner of "filling it in" exposes his or her patterns of experiencing in ways for which direct expression is utterly inadequate. For example, a guided fantasy might take the following form:

> Imagine yourself to be going down a corridor. You come to a door. You go through it and take the stairs to a room—*your* room. Describe that room and how you feel about it.

This fantasy has a number of potentially significant aspects toward which the therapist would pay close attention because they give clues about the client's individual style of experiencing.

One person described her scenario: The corridor was long, well-lighted, made of marble. She ran lightly down it. The door was open, inviting her further in. She went *up* the stairs to a large room that was furnished with antiques, marble statues, and plush, well-matched furniture. The room was a sitting room that opened out onto a sundeck, filled with a wide variety of healthy plants.

A second person saw herself walking down a short, dark, and damp corridor. The door was closed. She opened it with misgivings to stairs that took her *down* to a small, enclosed, and sparsely furnished bedroom, with no windows. She liked that room very much, feeling secure and comfortable in it.

The manner in which these two young women interpreted and

filled in the fantasy reveals something of how they relate to their worlds. The room was a personal, intimate place for each, suggested as the place in which they would most want to spend their time alone. While each of these women might have been able to articulate some of what they had shown through their "fantasy," they *showed* more than they could have described. The guided fantasy is a unique and provocative tool for the therapist interested in gaining needed information about a client's subjective experiencing. And the clients can also gain information about themselves in this exercise. In a group, they can listen to how others fill in the fantasy. Or therapists might tell clients about *their* room. Or they can use some other device to show clients how their descriptions are uniquely theirs and thus uniquely patterned.

One way in which the therapist could communicate this to the client is to gather further "evidence" of "how" the client is. For example, a female client may select a small, dark chair in a corner away from the light. She may have dreams in which themes of darkness and enclosure are prominent. She may wear dark clothes and sit crouched up, with her arms folded around her. She may desire a room that is womblike. When asked to draw a picture of a person, she might draw a very small person. That is, patterns that emerge in a fantasy intended to draw on the most intimate and personal aspects of a person's experiencing would emerge in other things that the client said or did. The therapist could simply provide observations on the commonalities among tasks and types of expression and ask the client to comment. This is close to a direct expression, however, and risks moving the client into a defensive posture.

Discussion

For Diane, the therapist could have used one or more of a number of techniques to mirror her to herself. Specifically, when she exhibited a tense and nervous style of relating to the situation, the therapist could have devised a way to show her to herself, rather than try to describe objectively what he had observed. For example, he could have taken on some of her mannerisms, playing the role of a nervous person until she recognized it as herself; or he could have asked *her* to play a nervous person until she saw that she had already been engaging in such a manner; or he could have constructed some sort of verbal device, such as a highly symbolic story or a less symbolic but more realistically detailed psychological portrait of herself. He might have "sculpted" her into a viscerally revealing position.

He might have asked her to describe a plant or animal that she feels represents her. He could have chosen a number of possibilities, simply taking care to keep the structure of whatever he used congruent to Diane's experiencing so that she could see herself in the similarity.

At any rate, indirect communication is a productive part of therapy. It can even be utilized effectively with clients who respond positively to straightforward verbal communication, if for no other reason than to maintain rapport and interest. There are many more techniques available than those described here, as rich and varied as the therapist's imagination. Like actors, therapists deliberately lay down limits and styles of life so that they can detect those that are undeliberately laid down by clients. They help the client "feel" his or her way to occluded boundaries that the client lives prethematically, prompting clients to speak to themselves about these boundaries and other possibilities for themselves. The therapist wants clients to try to see their personal and interpersonal situations from some point of view other than the one in which their problems are occurring. The "how" is the medium of change, and clients must see their current "how" in its problematic or inadequate form in order to change away from it—they must see that it is not a necessary reality for them. Therapy in this way amounts to "drawing close to whatever is basic for a person's consciousness" (Scott 1982, 158), helping the client to discover that consciousness in its complex of "how" and "what." With a deliberate metaphor in a protected setting, the therapist can "set traps" for the disclosure of experiencing that people will not acknowledge in ordinarily unprotected situations. Clients feel no need to keep their troublesome—and perhaps guilty—mode of experiencing hidden within their own shadows, because they are "only playing."

Kierkegaard's special contribution to therapy, then, begins with the double reflection. To overlook this aspect is to risk passing up the human sensitivity needed for metaphor construction in therapeutic intervention. His detailed analysis of the human condition, evident in psychological portraits of people in all manner of existing, aids in understanding the personal world of individuals that stands as background to their stated attitudes, beliefs, and overt behaviors. He points to the subjectively permeated objective world, reminding the therapist of the humanly lived situation involved in all aspects of the therapeutic exchange.

Indirect communication in any form avoids classification, generalization, and mediation. It engenders sensitivity to concreteness and uniqueness. The relationship that develops in a therapeutic setting that involves indirect communication incorporates styles of life, histories of awareness, qualities of attention, moods, commitments, disaffections, and predispositions in both the therapist and client such that they relate to each other in the fullness of their humanity. We saw much of this in the relationship that developed between Diane and her therapist. It goes on in all other responsible therapeutic interventions. The experienced and the experiencing of *both* are integral to what goes into and what comes out of the therapeutic process. Utilizing direct communication where appropriate, but seeing the place of indirect communication, will facilitate the goals of therapy—growth and change in the client—because the therapist is sensitive to the client's full experiential structure.

6
Conclusion

Diane was more deeply embedded than her therapist had suspected in her refusal to acknowledge reactions in herself that touched on sensitive areas. She persisted in denying that her relationship to her mother had anything to do with her daily nausea, her fear of commitment. Several times the therapist attempted to provoke an unguarded self-perception in Diane, to get her at least to see actual concrete behaviors that she exhibited yet failed to own. His efforts were continually frustrated.

He set up role-playing situations, with both Diane and himself (at different times) in the role of her mother. He used guided fantasies that he thought would allow Diane the free play she seemed to need to display herself without emotional commitment. He had her describe a possible scenario in which she sat home on a holiday instead of going, out of guilt-ridden sense of duty, to her mother's house. He even brought a phone into the room, instructing the secretary to make it ring, then told Diane it was her mother and she was *not* to answer the phone. He videotaped her response, confident that *this* mirror could not fail.

She trembled noticeably and played with the ring on her finger as she watched the phone. After awhile, the phone stopped ringing. Then the therapist showed Diane the videotape. She acknowledged what she saw on the tape with a noncommital shrug and gave a rational response: she thought that if her mother was calling her *there*, it must have been an emergency.

Finally, the therapist asked Diane to sit in on a few group sessions. The other members of the group were similarly blocked from integrated functional self-awareness, although he did not inform her of this. For several weeks Diane attended, listening to the others but making little comment. She mentioned in her own session to the therapist that the group seemed irrelevant to her situation. She failed to see why he had requested her attendance. The situations of the other members were not at all like hers, she pointed out: one man was dealing with a self-imposed feud with his son; a woman was addicted to a bad habit; and another woman was experiencing difficulties in feeling accepted by her colleagues. The therapist said nothing to Diane's complaint, but strongly suggested she continue to join the group.

One day, the therapist told the group the story of what had happened to him in his own group experience in graduate school (described in chapter 5). He detailed his stubborn attitude, then described the impact on him when the other group member had mirrored his expression and behavior. Diane listened attentively. Her face was serious while the others laughed at the irony of the therapist's discovery—his emotional denial of feeling emotion. She said nothing then, but admitted in her own session the next week that she had learned something; she had learned how it was possible, even commonplace, *not* to be aware of things one was doing. She related to the therapist that she had been watching a television program in full concentration when her sister had come into the room, approached her, and then made a face that showed Diane to herself: she had been so involved in the program that she had failed to feel the concentration expressed in her body and face that made her look so funny to another person.

From that point, Diane began to make progress in therapy. She was more open to her possible blindspots. Her willingness to see had been achieved via a metaphor intended for someone else, but one that had touched profoundly on her own situation as well. The therapist had not told Diane the story from graduate school because he had thought it a bit too obvious. With some clients the obvious works, while others are insulted. However, in telling the story to others in Diane's presence, it had been doubly removed from her, distanced enough to be nonthreatening.

Diane had, through her self-realization, been freed of the negative, hindering blockage that had been a wall between her and her therapist—step one in Kierkegaard's process. She had become open to doing the work that needed to be done, on her way to step two—growth.

Indirect communication is an important supplement to therapy, one which should be used when clients must be "approached from behind." It is appropriate—indeed, almost necessary!—for those who have falsified their experiencing and are blind to it, for those who overintellectualize and might be ready and quite able to put up a cognitively structured guard, and for those who are just simply too embarrassed to talk straightforwardly about their problem. Indirect communication should be brought in when the therapist has established firm trust and rapport and has become familiar enough with the client to hypothesize fairly accurately what has the best chance of working. Diane's therapist suspected, given the futility of his overt and covert attempts, that Diane needed even more distance than ordinary means of indirect communication allowed. He put her into the group, hoping for just such an opportunity to tell a story that was about her, metaphorically, but was not directed to her.

For Kierkegaard, indirect communication had been meant originally in a religious context, but it is based on a human developmental psychology (Pojman 1984). As such, it can be utilized for therapy without accepting religion as a necessary context. Kierkegaard intended with indirect communication to force people inward for self-understanding, for self-honesty, to utilize subjectively layered knowledge for more self-aware choices. He wanted them to hear their own inner voice, to awaken the sleeping spirit. Kierkegaard viewed subjectivity as a reliance on the inner flow of personal experiencing, a passionately involved manner of engaging in the world that involved will and decision to a high degree, but that was basically inaccessible to concepts and language. Any form of communication directed toward that part of human existence had to somehow embody, artistically, a fluid representation of that process. Kierkegaard ([1848] 1942) describes this with a metaphor:

> The military assumes that every country boy who joins the army possesses the necessary capacities to develop into a soldier. . . . Now the communication begins. The corporal doesn't explain to the soldier what it is to drill, etc.; he communicates it to him as an art. He teaches him to use the abilities and potential so that they are actualized. . . . The object of communication is consequently not an objective knowledge but a realization. (269)

In the Kierkegaardian model of communication, the figure/background structure of consciousness shows us the possibility that we can be unaware of part of what we experience. Nothing we can name will correspond to the immediacy of the flow of visceral experiencing, so if we concentrate on knowledge via language, we will inevitably lose something of ourselves. Unfortunately, the dominant bias in psychology is to do just that, and it filters down from theory to practice.

When knowledge is defined in strictly objective terms, that which is nonobjectifiable cannot, by definition, be "known." Gilbert Ryle (1966) claimed that everything is, in principle, knowable. While he admits that the act of knowing in the moment of its immediacy eludes knowledge, it is not privileged to escape forever; it becomes the target of a successive act of knowledge. If it is not hit by an ensuing act of knowledge, there is no substance to it. It can simply be dismissed.

Ryle's claim opposes the theme of this work, which proposes that immediacy is nonobjectifiable and will not be grasped fully even in a succeeding moment. Which position is correct? If the immediate moment cannot be grasped as it is happening, how can anyone really know if it is brought into focus as an object for reflection a moment later? If *it* eludes immediate specification, then perhaps—one cannot be sure—the subsequent moment of reflection *does* grasp it. This is an objection not only to Ryle's position but also to the approach evident throughout this work.

Contrary to Ryle, a great mass of clinical data indicates that successive acts of reflection systematically *miss* the "inner life." Diane's situation was not an isolated case. Many neuroses are situated in some degree of self-obscuring or blindness. What we claim to "grasp reflectively" as we "turn inward" is really a complex and precarious inference from what we take to be our behavior in the world. This inference is subject to all manner of breakdown. Diane may have thought she was perfectly composed at the time that she exhibited grossly nervous behaviors. Her inward perception was clearly distorted. Indeed, persons can reflect in such a way that insight is actually prevented: they can be too concerned about putting a name to everything, or they can shut out, on principle, whatever they cannot bring into the fold of explicit conscious awareness. This study indicates that this derives from an essential difficulty of the human condition—not merely from neurotic or psychotic distortions of self. Clinical data simply reveal gross processes of self-obscuration that run through human life. Diane's becoming aware of her scrunched-up expression of concentration when someone else showed it to her is an example that many people would recognize, and perhaps be able to add a similar, everyday illustration of their own.

It is evident from human behavior that people often do not grasp the immediate quality of their own experiencing; at least this is clear. Otherwise, they would be more aware of what they were doing and not prone to surprise about themselves. It may be objected that they are self-obscured simply because they prevent themselves from reflecting—perhaps they dimly sense that something unpleasant would be revealed to them if they took reflective note of their engagements. However, it seems clear from the mass of data available—and even from our own typical experiences of ourselves—that even when people do reflect, they often fail to grasp their own prior immediacies.

We can suppose, contrary to Cartesian subjectivism (Ryle's position is a version of this), that there is no mental substance that has the essential power to perceive its own perceiving, and thus no all-seeing homunculus within persons to show them fully to themselves. Rather, we view the qualities of prior immediacies as elusive to a reflecting consciousness, as Kierkegaard pointed out, and as distorted by its mediation, especially when gravely maladaptive behaviors go undetected by the person exhibiting them.

I am not claiming that consciousness never grasps the preceding immediacy at all. Instead, even when reflection functions as well as it can, the very idea of reflection, according to Husserl, necessitates that the reflected on be presented as *having been*: consciousness must grasp something of the preceding immediacy if reflection functions at all, but I question whether it is adequate to the task of capturing it in its fullness. (That it must grasp something of the preceding immediacy without alteration is an acceptable remnant of Cartesianism.)

But the major point is that even in those cases when conscious awareness was able to supply accurate "objective" knowledge of the immediate qualities of moments past—Diane was aware that she had made a drawing, that she had not wanted to do it, that she was relieved to have it done—such accuracy can still prevent one from *feeling* the very qualities about which one is being accurate. The qualitative difference between the actual experiencing and the subsequent reflecting on the experiencing points to the probability that a conscious, naming reflection is a mediating force that distorts, to some degree, the raw elements of experiencing. It is akin to being disappointed by an altogether inadequate photo of a breath-taking view.

Thus, one can intelligently maintain that reflection is defective, as has been indicated by some of the cases presented. If consciousness could fully grasp its own immediacy, then we would expect persons to be less self-obscured and less self-deceived than we often find them. That Diane could smoke five cigarettes and giggle nervously for fifteen minutes, then deny that she had done any such thing would seem to be impossible. It appears to be more difficult to be aware of how one is in the world than either Descartes or Ryle suppose. That we can be disengaged from our own experiencing is evident in the typical way in which people involve themselves in the world, and especially in the more pronounced cases of neurosis and psychosis.

In opposition to the Cartesian self-revelatory consciousness, Kierkegaardian *subjectivity* points to a prereflective consciousness that is absorbed in the world. There is no substance that can turn in

upon itself—no self-illuminating "chamber of mirrors." The qualities of this subjectivity are elusive to a reflecting consciousness that
turns the world into objects for itself. Although we say that consciousness turns in upon itself, this metaphor blinds us to the probability that the great mass of prereflective life—the great mass of
qualitative immediacy—eludes the conceptual meshes of self-
initiated reflection. Instead of saying that consciousness "turns in
upon itself," it would be better to say that it squints at a world-
involvement that it depletes and disrupts in the effort to arrest, and
that it misses the fullness and immediacy of itself.

If we choose to retain the optical metaphors of reflecting and mirroring, then we must say that the world in which we find ourselves
with others who are like us reflects and mirrors our immediacy in a
more nearly adequate way than does the fragmenting, stabilizing
mode of explicit consciousness. We can see ourselves in others, as
Diane saw herself in her sister, or Dostoevsky saw himself in the
Polish prisoner. It is this that best achieves *double* reflection: the
arresting confrontation with the gush of prereflective life just as it
eludes the meshes of self-initiated "outward" reflection. This argument rests on the empirical evidence of what people are actually
like, but it offers no definitive conclusion. To make a conclusive
statement about the nature of human experiencing is to ignore the
point that the evidence clearly reveals: that immediate experiencing
is not available to a naming consciousness, and thus it defies a description that is linguistically devised. That one cannot answer the
question of *what* the immediacy is does not prove to be a shortcom-
ing; to leave it as it is and seek other means of access to it is a
strength.

Ryle's position, as attractive as it is to those who want to believe
that all states of affairs are accessible to words-as-reference and thus
directly communicable, not only overestimates the self-illuminating
power of consciousness, but is an egregious begging of the questions
of both knowledge and reality. The circularity is obvious: reality
is objectively knowable—in some direct, literal, and perceptual
way—and anything that is not thus objectively knowable is not real.

Despite this circularity, many psychologists have championed this
conception of knowledge and of an objectively attainable reality.
Desiring to have psychological states of affairs laid out in clearly
defined terms, the professional psychologist has been strictly trained
toward objectivity, toward the categorization of all human phenomena. While objectivity itself is not a negative quality—it is
essential to comprehension, description, and verbal communication—it can and often does lead to the reductionistic approach of

objectivism. The products of an objective consciousness that fragments the world into discrete objects are thus viewed as the definitive totality of human reality, and the professional who works under
the assumptions of this bias works with an incomplete and distorted
conception of human phenomena. Only the experienc*ed* is made
explicit because the immediate experienc*ing* is not easily accessible
and is thus easy to ignore or forget altogether. The gaps left by this
restrictive focus are generally closed with some sort of intellectual
patchwork, akin to Ryle's circularity.

Had Diane's therapist seen only what she was doing and saying,
he would have been confused and would have failed to sense the
underlying currents of a subjectively obscured style of being in the
world that allows the possibility of such an apparent contradiction.
Without this glimpse, via his own double reflection, he would have
had few resources with which to deal with her.

Objectivism is a mode of conceptual organization—a way of
perceiving the world that results from human desire and purpose.
The set of premises that supports and promotes a strictly objective
outlook is given priority in explanatory schemas. However, this
approach assumes an all-encompassing consciousness that is unaware of its limitations. It is an activity that forgets itself *as* an activity that cannot subsume itself. A naming consciousness ignores
and then seals itself off from the elusive immediacy of its own
ongoing engagement. This blurring of its limitations is grounded in
the nature of a self that can forget itself. Diane exhibits this possibility on an individual level; at a community level, self-forgetting can
grow into theories that promote a partial picture of human existence
and reveal in themselves, by their very inception, the ludicrous
absent-mindedness that Kierkegaard points out: thinkers who
think themselves out of existence.

Being engulfed in immediate engagements, as Diane was, allows
humans to think and act without being explicitly aware of that thinking and/or acting. The lack of explicit awareness allows the possibility of a separation between the person and his or her activities that is
unobtrusive and thus unnoticed by the person. The philosophy of
objectivism encourages such separation, since facets of what a person *has* experienced are blocked-out in words, in statements, or in
theories that overshadow the inarticulate margins of the more fluid
experiencing. A community of thinkers that employs an objectivist
approach creates further opportunity for self-alienation as individual psychologists fuse their identities with that of the group, then
bring their own neglect into the therapeutic situation. They become
engulfed in the community orientation, contacting human life (even
their own) through general concepts until their tacit modes of in-

dividuality are gradually closed off without their being aware of it. Through this "absent-mindedness," objectivity as a quality of thought can develop into a self-deceptive perspective that depends on severing the thinker's thought from his or her subjective modes. Not only does this activity facilitate theories that fragment and partialize general human existence, but it blurs the perceptions of the practicing therapist, who in turn fails to gain a full sense of his or her clients. This state of affairs sets up a lack of sensitivity to clients who have falsified their existence through a process of disavowal, and further aggravates an already debilitating situation.

If the goal of psychology and thus of therapy is the apprehension (as much as possible) of the complete structure of human existence—especially for the purpose of assisting people away from dysfunction and toward psychological growth—losing the connection between the content of the experienc*ed* and the background flow of the experienc*ing* that penetrates the content hinders the achievement of this goal. Not only does the therapist work without a full awareness, but he or she inadvertently blocks self-awareness in their clients, which the clients need to move out of their problematic situation. To have viewed Diane only as a complex of symptoms to be looked up in the Diagnostic Statistical Manual III, or as an entity who exhibits contradictory behaviors, would have done nothing more than build an additional wall between Diane and that part of herself that she had closed off.

In general, clients are already separated from some aspect of their experiencing; they are involved in the world but not attuned to *how* they are involved. If they are approached on an explicitly conscious level by the therapist, they will likely be further alienated from themselves, since a therapist's overly objective stance presupposes some degree of self-alienation or neglect.

This progressive alienation can be circumvented, first, by recognizing the bias inherent in an approach that insists on drawing all human phenomena into verbal form; and, second, by acknowledging that such an approach is insufficient for a comprehensive assessment of, and relation to, the lived reality of human beings. Persons *can* be so engrossed in their attitudes or behavior that they actually cannot see the background from which the behavior emerges. Like Diane, like Paul, they may not be experiencing their experiences as fully as they could. We ought not view ourselves and each other through a perspective that conceals our actual experiencing. An approach that allows the use of objectivity in its place, as well as acknowledges the nonobjectifiable aspects of human existence, is in order.

Ironically, the very conditions for the self-deception described above allow Kierkegaard's ideas on double reflection and indirect communication their place in the therapeutic dynamic. People are self-obscured at the margins of consciousness, where clear boundaries fan out into decreasing awareness. This is where double reflection comes in, giving a glimpse of the flow of experiencing that feeds into more explicit engagements but that is typically in the shadows. Thus, the features of human consciousness that allow one to become fragmented, even to the point of yielding distorted theories about ourselves as a species, also provide a means of reintegration. Via double reflection, indirect communication is possible. Interpretations can be made at an individual level where concrete change is more accessible.

Such an approach expands the concepts of "knowledge" and "states of affairs" beyond objectivist boundaries. It admits to the ambiguous nature of human experience and acknowledges the need to mirror the experiencing rather than to cling to vain attempts to depict that experiencing in nonambiguous, verbal terms. Individuals can be presented with a meaning scheme that is structured isomorphically to their own lived situation—as when the therapist played the role of self-questioner for the family who needed to question themselves—so that they can "see" themselves, and can then be offered possibilities for reorganization of their perspective. Such an approach allows people to relive their situations imaginatively; the "as if" involvement reduces self-obliviousness and cuts through habitual defenses. A metaphorical device or relation that can display the self away from itself, while preserving the lived actuality of the experiencing of that self, allows a recognition to occur in a context that will be concretely meaningful to the individual involved. It produces a liberating psychological activity without necessitating actual movement in the world.

That which human beings hold in common provides the structure for this approach, as was noted in detail in chapter 3. Through shared human experiencing, one can grasp—to some extent—another's subjective modes of being in the world. That we are similar to one another allows us to be "metaphors" for one another—mirrors through which persons can view themselves.

This relation can be effectively and productively exploited in therapy. Using Kierkegaard's detailed analysis of indirect communication, one can detect the structure of the communication process. Therapists apprehend the client's experiencing through their own by double reflecting—by retaining an awareness of their own experiencing (how what they perceive strikes them) as an integral part of their thinking and observing. They then utilize their sense of the client to contrive a metaphorical device that will bypass direct (verbal and referential) communication yet still confront the client by startling him or her into a reciprocal double reflection. Indirect communication is then achieved through flexibly structured metaphor. That which has been but a prethematic part of the client's self is made evident to him—he is jolted into seeing it—as part of himself. This relation is analogous to when an actor, who "fleshes out" a type of human response to a situation, encourages personal resonance in an individual who is in a similar situation.

Since clients express themselves on levels that can be addressed objectively as well as on levels that cannot, therapists must use an approach that will respond to either mode of expression. They must also be able to make the intersection of "how" and "what" livable for the client. Since not all experiencing is captured in conscious reflection (the "first reflection" in Kierkegaard's schema), it is not directly expressible, and thus not verbally communicable. The communication of lived human immediacy must be indirect. That it *can* be communicated indicates the error of thinking that all states of affairs are objectifiable. That it must be communicated *indirectly* should prompt the therapist to develop skills in this area. If the communication of facts and information is combined with the communication of subjectivity, the therapist can gain a broad base from which to diagnose and treat the client's situation.

One question about indirect communication that must still be addressed is that of the ethics of the procedure. Kierkegaard calls it a sort of deception, but a deception in the name of truth. Since, he believed, it is our duty to bear witness to the truth, a deception in this sense seems justified in his mind.

But one must ask, are therapists really showing the clients to themselves, or are they manipulating them into seeing something that they want them to see? One answer is that indirect communication, unlike other forms of therapy, has little capacity for "talking someone into something." If the stories, roles, mirroring postures ring true, clients will resonate to them. If not, they probably will just shrug.

On the other hand, what gives anyone the right to be such a midwife, to raise another's consciousness? Socrates was put to death for such activity. Therapists might say that clients have come to them for therapy, and this is what is involved. But what if the "message" is misinterpreted? What if the client chooses badly as a result? What if he kills himself? The same questions can be asked of more traditional forms of therapy. There is always risk in guiding people, in helping, in facilitating change. To all the ethical questions challeng-

ing the use of indirect communication, one might reply, is it ethical
not to do what is in one's power if there is the possibility of positive
change? Should therapists simply abandon clients to their debilitating self-blindness? It is a matter for thought for advocates on both
sides. Clearly, indirect communication cannot be dismissed lightly,
either on therapeutic terms or on ethical terms.

References

Anderson, Raymond E. 1970. "Kierkegaard's Theory of Communication." In *Kierkegaard's Presence in Contemporary American Life: Essays from Various Disciplines*, edited by Lewis A. Lawson, 206–29. Metuchen, N.J.: Scarecrow Press.

Armstrong, Paul B. 1981. "Reading Kierkegaard—Disorientation and Reorientation." In *Kierkegaard's Truth: The Disclosure of the Self*, edited by Joseph H. Smith, 23–50. New Haven: Yale University Press.

Atwood, George E., and Robert D. Stolorow. 1977 "The Life and Work of Wilhelm Reich: A Case Study of the Subjectivity of Personality Theory." *The Psychoanalytic Review* 64: 5–20.

———. 1984. *Structures of Subjectivity: Explorations in Psychoanalytic Phenomenology*. Hillsdale, N.J.: The Analyic Press.

Atwood, George, and Silvan S. Tomkins. 1976. "On the Subjectivity of Personality Theory." *Journal of the History of the Behavioral Sciences* 12:166–77.

Bandler, R., and J. Grinder. 1979. *Frogs into Princes*. Moab, Utah: Real People Press.

Barker, Philip. 1985. *Using Metaphors in Psychotherapy*. New York: Bruner/Mazel.

Beardsley, Monroe C. 1981. "The Metaphorical Twist." In *Philosophical Perspectives on Metaphor*, edited by Mark Johnson, 105–22. Minneapolis: University of Minnesota Press.

Becker, E. 1973. *Denial of Death*. New York: Macmillan.

Bejerholm, Lars. 1980. "Communication." In *Concepts and Alternatives in Kierkegaard*, edited by Marie M. Thulstrup, 52–59. Copenhagen: C. A. Reitzels Boghandel.

Belkin, Gary S. 1980. *Contemporary Psychotherapies*. Chicago: Rand McNally.

Bergman, Joel S. 1982. "Paradoxical Interventions with People Who Insist on Acting Crazy." *American Journal of Psychotherapy* 36 (April):214–22.

Bernstein, Richard J. 1983. *Beyond Objectivism and Relativism: Science, Hermeneutics and Praxis*. Philadelphia: University of Pennsylvania Press.

Binkley, Timothy. 1981. "On the Truth and Probity of Metaphor." In *Philosophical Perspectives on Metaphor*, edited by Mark Johnson, 136–53. Minneapolis: University of Minnesota Press.

Binswanger, Ludwig. 1956. "Existential Analysis and Psychotherapy." In *Progress in Psychotherapy*, edited by Frieda Fromm-Reichman and Jo Moreno, 139–152. New York: Grune and Stratton.

———. 1958. "The Case of Ellen West," translated by Werner M. Mendel and Joseph Lyons. In *Existence: A New Dimension in Psychiatry and Psychology*, edited by Rollo May, Ernest Angel, and Henri F. Ellenberger, 237–364. New York: Basic Books.

————. 1958. "The Existential Analysis School of thought," translated by Ernest Angel. In *Existence: A New Dimension in Psychiatry and Psychology*, edited by Rollo May, Ernest Angel, and Henri F. Ellenberger, 191–213. New York: Basic Books.

Black, Max. 1981. "Metaphor." In *Philosophical Perspectives on Metaphor*, edited by Mark Johnson, 63–82. Minneapolis: University of Minnesota Press.

Burstow, Bonnie. 1980–81. "A Critique of Binswanger's Existential Analysis." *Review of Existential Psychology and Psychiatry* 17:245–52.

Caputo, John D. 1982. "Hermeneutics as the Recovery of Man." *Man and World* 15:343–67.

Caputo, John D. 1983. "The Thought of Being and the Conversation of Mankind: The Case of Heidegger and Rorty." *Review of Metaphysics* 36:661–85.

Collingwood, R. G. 1951. *The Idea of History*. London: Oxford University Press.

Collins, James. 1981. "Kierkegaard's Imagery of the Self." In *Kierkegaard's Truth: The Disclosure of the Self*, edited by Joseph H. Smith, 51–84. New Haven: Yale University Press.

Cornelius, Benjamin A. 1965. *Science, Technology and Human Values*. Columbia: University of Missouri Press.

Crites, Stephen. 1972. "Pseudonymous Authorship as Art and as Act." In *Kierkegaard: A Collection of Critical Essays*, edited by Josiah Thompson, 183–229. Garden City, N.Y.: Anchor Books.

Davidson, Donald. 1981. "What Metaphors Mean." In *Philosophical Perspectives on metaphor*, edited by Mark Johnson, 200–220. Minneapolis: University of Minnesota Press.

Dennett, Daniel C. 1978. *Brainstorms: Philosophical Essays on Mind and Psychology*. Montgomery, Vt.: Bradford Books.

Descartes, Rene. 1969. *The Philosophical Works of Descartes*, translated by Elizabeth S. Haldane and G. R. T. Ross, vol. 1. Cambridge: Cambridge University Press.

Deutscher, Max. 1983. *Subjecting and Objecting*. Oxford: Basil Blackwell.

Dilts, Robert, J. Grinder, R. Bandler, and J. Delozier. 1980. *The Study of the Structure of Subjective Experience*. Cupertino, Calif.: Meta Publications.

Dostoevsky, F. M. [1876] 1979. *The Diary of a Writer*. Translated by Boris Brasol. Santa Barbara, Calif.: Peregrine Smith.

Dummett, Michael. 1978. *Truth and Other Enigmas*. London: Gerald Duckworth.

Einstein, Albert. 1950. *Out of My Later Years*. New York: The Wisdom Library.

Ellis, Albert. 1958. "Rational Psychotherapy." *The Journal of General Psychology* 59:34–49.

————. 1962. *Reason and Emotion in Psychotherapy*. New York: Lyle Stuart.

Erickson, Milton. 1980. *Innovative Psychotherapy*. Vol. 4 of *Collected Papers*, edited by E. L. Rossi. New York: Irvington.

Evans, C. Stephen. 1977. *Preserving the Person*. Downer's Grove, Ill.: Intervarsity Press.

————. 1978. *Subjectivity and Religious Belief*. Grand Rapids, Mich.: Christian University Press.

————. 1983. *Kierkegaard's "Fragments" and "Postscript": The Religious Philosophy of Johannes Climacus*. Atlantic Highlands, N.J.: Humanities Press.

Fingarette, Herbert. 1963. *The Self in Transformation*. New York: Basic Books.

———. 1969. *Self-Deception*. New York: Humanities Press.

Frank, Joseph. 1983. *Dostoevsky: The Years of Ordeal, 1850–1859*. Princeton: Princeton University Press.

Frege, Gottlob. 1970. "On Sense and Reference," translated by Max Black. In *Translations from the Philosophical Writings of Gottlob Frege*, edited by Peter Geach and Max Black, 56–78. Oxford: Basil Blackwell.

Freud, Sigmund. [1914] 1957. "On the History of the Psychoanalytic Movement." In *Standard Edition*, 14:7–66. London: Hogarth Press.

———. [1925] 1959. "An Autobiographical Study." In *Standard Edition*, 20:7–74. London: Hogarth Press.

———. [1939] 1964. "Moses and Monotheism: Three Essays." In *Standard Edition*, 23:6–137. London: Hogarth Press.

Geha, Richard. 1983. On psychoanalytic history and the 'real' story of fictitious lives. Typescript.

Giorgi, Amedeo. 1970. *Psychology as a Human Science*. New York: Harper and Row.

Glasser, William. 1965. *Reality Therapy: A New Approach to Psychiatry*. New York: Harper and Row.

Goodman, Nelson. 1978. *Ways of World-Making*. Indianapolis, Ind.: Hackett.

Gordon, David. 1978. *Therapeutic Metaphors*. Cupertino, Calif.: Meta Publications.

Grice, H. P. 1961. "The Causal Theory of Perception." *Proceedings of the Aristotelian Society* 35:121–54.

Haley, J. 1973. *Uncommon Therapy*. New York: Norton.

Hannay, Alastair. 1979. "The 'What' and the 'How.'" In *Body, Mind and Method*, edited by D. F. Gustafson and B. L. Tapscott, 17–36. Boston: D. Reidel.

———. 1982. *Kierkegaard: The Arguments of the Philosophers*. Boston: Routledge and Kegan Paul.

Hegel, G. W. F. [1807] 1964. *The Phenomenology of Mind*. 2d ed., translated by Sir James Baillie. London: George Allen and Unwin.

Hempel, C. 1959. "The Function of General Laws in History." In *Theories of History*, edited by P. Gardiner, 344–56. New York: Free Press.

Henle, Paul. 1981. "Metaphor." In *Philosophical Perspectives on Metaphor*, edited by Mark Johnson, 83–104. Minneapolis: University of Minnesota Press.

Herink, Richie, ed. 1980. *The Psychotherapy Handbook*. New York: New American Library.

Hillman, J. 1975. "The Fiction of Case History: A Round." In *Religion as Story*, edited by J. Wiggins, 123–73. New York: Harper and Row.

Holmer, Paul. 1981. "Post-Kierkegaard: Remarks about Being a Person." In *Kierkegaard's Truth: The Disclosure of the Self*, edited by Joseph H. Smith, 3–22. New Haven: Yale University Press.

Husserl, Edmund. 1970. *The Crisis of European Sciences and Transcendental Phenomenology*. Translated by David Carr. Evanston, Ill.: Northwestern University Press.

Ihde, Don. 1977. *Experimental Phenomenology*. New York: G. P. Putnam's Sons.

Johnson, Mark. "Introduction: Metaphor in the Philosophical Tradition." In *Phi-*

losophical Perspectives on Metaphor, edited by Mark Johnson, 3–47. Minneapolis: University of Minnesota Press.

Johnson, Ralph Henry. 1972. *The Concept of Existence in the "Concluding Unscientific Postscript."* The Hague: Martinus Nijhoff.

Kelly, George. 1955. *The Psychology of Personal Constructs*. Vol. 1. New York: Norton.

Kierkegaard, Søren. [comp. 1834–55] 1942. *Soren Kierkegaard's Journals and Papers*. Vols. 1 and 4. Translated and edited by Howard V. Hong and Edna H. Hong. Bloomington: Indiana University Press.

———. [1843] 1971. *Either/Or*. Vols. 1 and 4. Translated by D. F. and L. M. Swenson. Princeton: Princeton University Press.

———. [1846] 1968. *Concluding Unscientifiic Postscript*. Translated by David F. Swenson and Walter Lowrie. Princeton: Princeton University Press, 1968.

———. [1847] 1962. *Works of Love*. Translated by Howard V. Hong and Edna H. Hong. New York: Harper and Row.

———. [1850] 1941. *Training in Christianity*. Translated by Walter Lowrie. Princeton: Princeton University Press.

———. [1859] 1962. *The Point of View for My Work as an Author*. Translated by Walter Lowrie. Edited by Benjamin Nelson. New York: Harper and Row.

Lakoff, George, and Mark Johnson. 1981. "Conceptual Metaphor in Everyday Language." In *Philosophical Perspectives on Metaphor*, edited by Mark Johnson, 286–325. Minneapolis: University of Minnesota Press.

Lankton, S., and C. Lankton. 1983. *The Answer Within*. New York: Brunner/Mazel.

Lerner, Arthur, ed. 1978..*Poetry in the Therapeutic Experience*. New York: Pergamon Press.

Mackey, Louis. 1971. *Kierkegaard: A Kind of Poet*. Philadelphia: University of Pennsylvania Press.

———. 1981. "A Ram in the Afternoon: Kierkegaard's Discourse of the Other." In *Kierkegaard's Truth: The Disclosure of the Self*, edited by Joseph H. Smith, 193–234. New Haven: Yale University Press.

Macquarrie, John. 1972. *Existentialism*. New York: Penguin Books.

Maslow, Abraham. 1966. *The Psychology of Science*. Chicago: Henry Regnery.

May, Rollo. 1958. "The Origins and Significance of the Existential Movement in Psychology." In *Existence: A New Dimension in Psychiatry and Psychology*, edited by Rollo May, Ernest Angel, and Henri F. Ellenberger, 3–36. New York: Basic Books.

Meissner, W. W. "Subjectivity in Psychoanalysis." In *Kierkegaard's Truth: The Disclosure of the Self*, edited by Joseph H. Smith, 267–312. New Haven: Yale University Press.

Menninger, Karl. 1958. *Theory of Psychoanalytic Technique*. New York: Basic Books.

Merleau-Ponty, M. 1962. *Phenomenology of Perception*. Translated by Colin Smith. London: Routledge and Kegan Paul.

Murray, Edward L. 1975. "The Phenomenon of the Metaphor: Some Theoretical Considerations." In *Duquesne Studies in Phenomenological Psychology*, edited by A. Giorgi, C. Fischer, and E. Murray, 2:281–300. Pittsburgh, Penn.: Duquesne University Press.

Nagel, E. 1961. *The Structure of Science: Problems in the Logic of Scientific Explanation*. New York: Harcourt, Brace and World.

Nagel, Thomas. 1979. *Mortal Questions*. Cambridge: Cambridge University Press.

Nielson, Harry. 1982. "Two Levels of Indirect Communication." In *Kierkegaard: Resources and Results*, edited by Alastair Mckinnon, 92–104. Montreal: Wilfrid Laurier University Press.

Nordentoft, Kresten. 1972. *Kierkegaard's Psychology*. Translated by Bruce Kirmmse. Pittsburgh, Penn.: Duquesne University Press.

Papp, P. 1982. "Staging Reciprocal Metaphors in a Couples Group." In *Dimensions of Family Therapy*, edited by M. Andolfi and I. Zwerling. New York: Guilford Press.

Perls. F. 1969. *Gestalt Therapy Verbatim*. Moab, Utah: Real People Press.

Polanyi, Michael. 1964. *Personal knowledge: Towards a Post-Critical Philosophy*. New York: Harper and Row.

Pojman, Louis. 1984. *The Logic of Subjectivity: Kierkegaard's Philosophy of Religion*. University: University of Alabama Press.

Reyna, L. J. 1964. "Conditioning Therapies, Learning Theory, and Research." In *The Conditioning Therapies*, edited by J. Wolpe, A. Salter, and L. J. Reyna, 169–80. New York: Holt, Rinehart and Winston.

Ricoeur, Paul. 1970. *Freud and Philosophy: An Essay on Interpretation*. Translated by Denis Savage. New Haven: Yale University Press.

————. 1981. "The Metaphorical Process as Cognition, Imagination, and Feeling." In *Philosophical Perspectives on Metaphor*, edited by Mark Johnson, 228–47. Minneapolis: University of Minnesota Press.

Rosen, S., ed. 1982. *My Voice Will Go with You: The Teaching Tales Of Milton H. Erickson*. New York: Norton.

Russell, Bertrand. 1959. *The Problems of Philosophy*. New York: Oxford University Press.

Ryle, Gilbert. 1966. *The Concept of Mind*. London: Hutchinson.

Salter, Andrew. 1964. "The Theory and Practice of Conditioned Reflex Therapy." In *The Conditioning Therapies*, edited by J. Wolpe, A. Salter, and L. J. Reyna, 21–37. New York: Holt, Rinehart and Winston.

Scheffler, Israel. 1982. *Science and Subjectivity*. 2d ed. Indianapolis, Ind.: Hackett.

Schultz, Duane. 1975. *A History of Modern Psychology*. 2d ed. New York: Academic Press.

Scott, Charles. 1982. *Boundaries in Mind*. New York: Crossroad.

Searle, John R. 1981. "Metaphor." In *Philosophical Perspectives on Metaphor*, edited by Mark Johnson, 248–87. Minneapolis: University of Minnesota Press.

Shmueli, Adi. 1971. *Kierkegaard and Consciousness*. Translated by Naomi Handelman. Princeton: Princeton University Press.

Sontag, Frederick. 1980. "The Role of Repetition." In *Concepts and Alternatives in Kierkegaard*, edited by Marie M. Thulstrup, 283–94. Copenhagen: C. A. Reitzels Boghandel.

Spence, Donald. 1982. *Narrative Truth and Historical Truth: Meaning and Interpretation in Psychoanalysis*. New York: Norton.

Stack, George J. 1976. *On Kierkegaard: "Philosophical Fragments"*. Atlantic Highlands, N.J.: Humanities Press.

Stainbrook, Edward. 1978. "Poetry and Behavior in the Psychotherapeutic Experience." In *Poetry in the Therapeutic Experience*, edited by Arthur Lerner, 1–11. New York: Pergamon Press.

Strickland, Ben. 1970. "Kierkegaard and Counseling for Individuality." In *Kierkegaard's Presence in Contemporary American Life: Essays from Various Disciplines*, edited by Lewis A. Lawson, 230–39. Metuchen, N.J.: Scarecrow Press.

Taylor, Mark C. 1980. *Journeys to Selfhood: Hegel and Kierkegaard*. Berkeley and Los Angeles: University of California Press.

Thomas, J. Heywood. 1957. *Subjectivity and Paradox*. Oxford: Basil Blackwell.

Wallas, Lee. 1985. *Stories for the Third Ear*. New York: Norton.

Warnock, Mary. 1976. *Imagination*. Berkeley and Los Angeles: University of California Press.

Watzlawick, Paul. 1978. *The Language of Change*. New York: Basic Books.

Watzlawick, Paul, J. H. Beavin, and D. D. Jackson. 1967. *Pragmatics of Human Communication*. New York: Norton.

Weber, Samuel. 1982. *The Legend of Freud*. Minneapolis: University of Minnesota Press.

Weeks, Gerald, and Luciano L'Abate. 1982. *Paradoxical Psychotherapy*. New York: Brunner/Mazel.

Wilk, J. 1985. "Ericksonian Therapeutic Patterns: a Pattern which Connects." In *Clinical Applications*, Vol. 2 of *Ericksonian Psychotherapy*, edited by J. Zeig. New York: Brunner/Mazel.

Wilshire, Bruce. 1970. "Kierkegaard's Theory of Knowledge and New Directions in Psychology and Psychoanalysis." In *Kierkegaard's Presence in Contemporary American Life: Essays from Various Disciplines*, edited by Lewis A. Lawson, 43–59. Metuchen, N.J.: Scarecrow Press.

———. 1982. *Role Playing and Identity: The Limits of Theatre as Metaphor*. Bloomington: Indiana University Press.

Wolpe, Joseph. 1964. "The Comparative Clinical Status of Conditioning Therapies and Psychoanalysis." In *The Conditioning Therapies*, edited by J. Wolpe, A. Salter, and L. J. Reyna, 5–20. New York: Holt, Rinehart, and Winston.

Zeig, J. 1980. *A Teaching Seminar with Milton H. Erickson, M. D*. New York: Brunner/Mazel.

Index

"Absentmindedness," 20–21, 45, 49, 121
Abstraction, 21, 27, 46–48, 50–51, 53, 54, 58, 64, 71, 76, 77, 99
Abstract thinker, 47, 51, 53, 76
Actuality, 51, 52, 53, 63, 76, 100, 122
Ad hominem, 50
Adler, Alfred, 102
Ambiguity of existence, 61–64, 66, 96, 99, 122
Archimedean Point, 19, 25

Barker, Philip, 14–15, 17, 18, 23, 66, 68, 104–5
Befindlichkeit, 78
Behaviorism, 34–36, 38, 39, 41, 42
Being-in-the-world, 36, 37, 38, 78
Binswanger, Ludwig, 30–31, 36–39, 52, 93–94
Biocentric Therapy, 34
Bookbinder, Hilarius, 87

Choreography, therapeutic, 105
Classical conditioning, 34
Climacus, Johannes, 87, 88
Cognitive-dynamic theories, 32–33
Concept of Mind, The, 43
Concluding Unscientific Postscript, 75, 80
Consciousness, 39, 41, 43, 50; content of, 27–28, 38; embodied, 61–62; intentional, 27, 28, 38, 52, 61; as introspection, 36–37; marginal, 16, 17, 27, 28, 62, 63, 69, 118–19; reflective, 16, 17, 21, 27, 28, 36, 44, 48, 54, 62, 89, 118, 120, 123; structure of, 16–17, 27–28; structuring, 27–28, 71, 89, 120; subconscious (unconscious), 30, 63, 69

Descartes, René, 43, 53, 117–18
De Silentio, Johannes, 87
Diagnostic Statistical Manual III, 121
Dialectic of subjectivity and objectivity, 28, 51–52, 53, 54–55, 61, 72, 84, 92–100, 112
Diane, the case of, 59–60, 64, 72–74, 78–79, 83, 84, 90, 94–101, 111–15, 118, 120, 121
"Diapsalmata," 87
Disavowal, 95, 121
Dostoevsky, Fyodor, 13–15, 22, 81, 119
Double reflection, 21, 23, 47, 55, 72, 75–80, 85, 86, 93, 96, 98–101, 105–6, 119, 120, 122–23

Either/Or, 87, 88
Ellis, Albert, 32–33, 38
Empirical concepts, 27, 34, 99
Enactment, 14, 65–66, 67, 71
Eremita, Victor, 87
Erickson, Milton, 17, 68–69, 72, 106–7, 110
Evans, C. Stephen, 21, 47, 52, 77, 79–80, 82, 86, 88
Existence, 93

Family sculpting, 105
Figure-background, 16, 70, 106–7
Fingarette, Herbert, 45, 96
Frege, Gottlob, 26
Freud, Sigmund, 29–32, 48

Genetic Fallacy, 50
Gestalt Therapy, 16, 69–70, 106–7
Glasser, William, 32
Goals of therapy, 20, 121
Grice, H. P., 91
Guided fantasy, 110–11

Hamlet, 65, 89
Haufniensis, Vigilius, 87
Hegel, G. W. F., 45, 46–47
Heidegger, Martin, 36, 78
"How," the: as blocked, 16–18, 28, 36; as dialectic with the "what," 38–39, 54, 56–60, 61, 80, 92–100, 112, 123;

disclosing of, 22, 23; as the "experiencing," 22, 73, 78, 87, 91, 93; as the
medium of change, 112; as visceral,
19, 80, 83. *See also* Subjectivity
Human possibility, 21, 23, 31, 37, 51,
52, 56–74, 76–78, 87–91, 95, 96, 97,
100, 122
Husserl, Edmund, 118
Hypnotic Therapy, 17, 69

Imagery, 19, 89–90, 106
Imagination, 67, 89–90, 122
Immediacy: as addressed by Ryle, 116–
17. *See also* Subjectivity
Implicit expression, 90–91
Implosive Therapy, 34
Indirect Communication, 81–91;
Erickson's use of, 68–69, 106–7; as
imagery, 19, 89–90; and implicit
expression, 90–91; as irony, 101; as
metaphor, 15, 18, 22, 66–68, 85, 107–
11, 123; as mirroring, 18, 20–22, 66–
68, 74, 85–86, 111–12; negative step,
83, 115; and nonverbal communication, 91; and paradox, 101–2; positive
step, 83, 115; in the pseudonyms, 67–
68, 86–89; and repetition, 83–84; and
role-playing, 103–7; in therapy, 68–
69, 98–113, 115–16, 122–24; as
visceral, 83, 112
Intentional thought, 27, 28, 38, 52, 61
Introspectionism, 36–37
Inwardness. *See* Subjectivity
Irony, 86, 101, 102
Isomorphism, 106, 108–9, 112, 123

Kant, Immanuel, 53, 90
Kierkegaard, Søren: on double reflection, 21–22, 72, 75–81, 103, 106, 122–
24; and Gestalt, 69–70, 106–7; on
Hegel's system, 46–47, 75; on human
reality, 87–88, 103; on indirect communication, 20–23, 66, 70, 72, 75–91,
96, 106–7, 116, 122–24; on objectivity and objectivism, 19, 20, 21, 22, 23,
40, 46, 49–51, 76–77; the pseudonyms, 67, 86–89; on self-deception,
47–48, 75–78, 100, 118, 120; on
subjectivity, 21–22, 61, 75–90,
97–100, 118–19
Knowledge: by acquaintance, 49;

human involvement in, 48–50;
second-order, 49; subjective, 54;
third-order, 49

"Leap of faith," 79
Linguistic communication (direct), 17,
19–22, 26–28, 38, 42, 46, 58, 60, 61,
62, 64, 72, 80–81, 85, 91, 92, 119; as
involved in self-deception, 57, 75–78,
92, 96–97, 123
Lived experiencing, 16, 17, 19–23, 62,
65, 72, 76, 91–94, 96, 98, 106, 123.
See also Subjectivity
Logical Positivism, 34, 39

Maieutic, 81–82
Maslow, Abraham, 51
May, Rollo, 41–42, 52, 93
Meaning, 26, 37, 48, 63, 86–87, 89–90,
122
Meaning matrix, 37, 38, 59, 60, 71, 94
Megavitamin Therapy, 34
Merleau-Ponty, Maurice, 61
Metaphor, 15, 18, 21, 22, 23, 56–74, 85,
87, 100, 119, 122–23; as guided fan-
tasy; 110–11; people as, 122; physi-
ognomic, 65, 103, 105, 108; theatri-
cal, 65, 108, 123; verbal, 107–11
Mimetic attunement, 62–70, 98, 99
Mimetic symbol, 18, 22, 63–70, 95
Mirroring, 18, 19, 20, 22, 55, 64–67, 74,
87–88, 95, 98–99, 119, 122–23; in
role-playing, 104–7
Modes of organization (psychological),
48–49, 79

Nagel, Thomas, 24, 42, 53
Natural science, 24–27, 29, 30, 33, 35,
44, 45, 47, 51–52, 62
Neurolinguistic Programming, 69,
107–8
Nonverbal communication, 91
Nordentoft, Kresten, 82

Objective bias, 28, 29, 40–41, 44, 119–
20
Objective observer, 24, 35, 39, 120, 121
Objective reflection, 27, 28, 42–43,
117–19, 123
Objectivism, 20, 24–29, 35–36, 38–55,
119–20, 122

Objectivity: as abstraction, 32, 44, 50, 53–54, 77–78; block to subjectivity, 21–23, 40, 44, 49, 53, 80, 118–21; as control, 29, 44–46; as dialectic, 38, 51–52, 54–55, 61, 72, 84, 92–100, 112; as human construct, 29, 44–46, 48–49; as knowledge, 24–40; as mediation, 41, 53; preference for, 28–40, 45–46, 49; in psychological theory, 24–55; reflection, 28, 53–54, 76–78, 99, 119; as self-deception, 44–46, 47–48, 80, 95, 117, 118; as systematic categorization, 31–38; in therapy, 29–40, 46–47, 53–55, 73; various views of, 24–29; as verbal labeling, 19, 28, 53–54, 76–77
Operant conditioning, 34

Paradox (in therapy), 101–3
Paul, the case of, 56–57, 60, 61, 63, 70, 84, 101, 104
Perception, 27, 62
Perls, F., 69–70
Personal Construct Therapy, 33–34
Phenomenal world, 24, 58
Phenomenology, 107
Professional community, 27–29, 34, 44–45, 48, 120
Pseudonyms, the, 67, 86–89, 106
Psychoanalysis, 29–32, 48, 49
Psychological theories: Behaviorism, 35–36, 38, 39, 41, 42; Gestalt, 69–70, 106–7; Introspectionism, 36–37; Neurolinguistic Programming, 69, 107–8; Personal Construct Therapy, 33–34; Psychoanalysis, 29–32, 48, 49; Rational-Emotive Therapy, 32–33; Reality Therapy, 32

Rational-Emotive Therapy (RET), 32–33
Reality Therapy, 32
Repetition, 83–84, 87
Role-playing, 22, 103–7
Ryle, Gilbert, 43, 116–20

Seduction Theory, 30

Self-awareness, 20, 22, 23, 58, 62, 70–72, 78, 82, 85–86, 90, 99, 116
Self-blindness, 14, 15, 16, 20, 21, 22, 23, 40, 44–46, 49, 51, 54, 57–58, 60, 63–64, 70–74, 76, 78–79, 83, 94–100, 117, 120–22
Self-deception. *See* Self-blindness
"Self talk," 33, 38
Socrates, 81–82
Socratic maieutic, 81–82
Spheres of existence (Kierkegaardian), 87–89
Subconscious, 30, 63, 69
Subjectivism, 52–53, 117–18
Subjectivity: as background for objectivity, 21–22, 28, 40–41, 49–55; as blocked by objectivity, 21–23, 40, 44, 49, 53, 80, 118–21; as dialectic, 28, 51–52, 54–55, 61, 72, 84, 92–100, 112; difficulty of describing, 60; as distinct from objectivity, 25, 51, 54–55, 61; as human point of view, 20, 39, 44, 58; as inwardness, 22, 58, 76, 81, 122; as lived immediacy, 17, 19, 22–23, 27, 36, 41–43, 52, 54, 57, 76–78, 81, 85–86, 97–100, 118–19; as personal involvement in the world, 21–22, 58–59, 83, 118–19; in therapy, 36–39, 52, 66–67, 70, 72–74, 92–113, 122–24; as visceral, 22, 58, 83
Systematic Desensitization, 34

"Teaching tales," 17, 68–69, 106
Theatrical metaphors, 65, 71, 108, 123

Unconscious. *See* Subconscious

"What," the, 22, 40; as dialectic with the "how," 38–39, 54, 56–60, 61, 80, 92–100, 112, 123; experiential content, 16–18, 22, 40; as reflective thought, 17, 22, 39; as verbal communication, 19, 28, 60. *See also* Objectivity
Wilshire, Bruce, 27, 62–70
Wundt, Wilhelm, 36–37